99 Musings *of a* Dogeared Pilgrim

99 Musings *of a* Dogeared Pilgrim

Daily Readings for Encouragement along the Way

JOHN COX

RESOURCE *Publications* • Eugene, Oregon

99 MUSINGS OF A DOGEARED PILGRIM
Daily Readings for Encouragement along the Way

Copyright © 2022 John Cox. All rights reserved. Except for brief quotations in critical publications or reviews, no part of this book may be reproduced in any manner without prior written permission from the publisher. Write: Permissions, Wipf and Stock Publishers, 199 W. 8th Ave., Suite 3, Eugene, OR 97401.

Resource Publications
An Imprint of Wipf and Stock Publishers
199 W. 8th Ave., Suite 3
Eugene, OR 97401

www.wipfandstock.com

PAPERBACK ISBN: 978-1-6667-3701-1
HARDCOVER ISBN: 978-1-6667-9604-9
EBOOK ISBN: 978-1-6667-9605-6

MARCH 2, 2022 12:20 PM

Bible extracts are taken from THE HOLY BIBLE, NEW INTERNATIONAL VERSION®, NIV® Copyright © 1973, 1978, 1984, 2011 by Biblica, Inc.® Used by permission. All rights reserved worldwide.

Dedicated to Yvonne,
my mother,
who died when we were both far too young.

Still remembered, never forgotten.

Contents

1	Burnt Toast and Marmalade	1
2	Ashes into Gemstones	3
3	Fear Not	5
4	Time	7
5	It's Unbelievable	9
6	Easter—Every Day	11
8	Disillusionment	15
9	Reality Check	17
10	Passion	20
11	Imagine	22
12	God—in Human Form	24
13	What Now?	26
14	Encouragement	30
15	Freedom	32
16	Organic Church	34
17	No Doubt About It	37
18	Dead and Alive	40
19	Together We Thrive	42
20	Jesus Makes a Difference	44
21	Praying	46

22	Not Much is More Than Enough	48
23	Learning from Nature	50
24	Gardening and Fences	52
25	Thanksgiving	55
26	Mindsets	58
27	Stay with It	60
28	Dark Days	62
29	Beyond My Comfort Zone	65
30	Character	68
31	On Fire	70
32	Plans	72
33	Investing	75
34	Easter	77
35	Power	80
36	Dinner at Simon's House	82
37	Ask and Receive	85
38	Facing Fear	87
39	Overcoming Timidity	90
40	Dare to Try	93
41	Why Church?	95
42	Never Insignificant	98
43	The Impact of Jesus	100
44	God's Green Fingers	103
45	Faith and Money	106
46	Ready, or Not?	108
47	Community	111
48	Three Strings	113
49	God's Olympics	116
50	Hitchhiking	118

51	A Taste of Heaven	120
52	Joy	122
53	Orphans No Longer	125
54	God's Spirit in Us	127
55	Declarations amid Despair	130
56	More Than Able	133
57	Forty Days	135
58	Like a Lion	138
59	Pilgrimage	140
60	God with Us	142
61	Extraordinary Wrapped in Ordinary	144
62	Following Jesus	147
63	Advent	149
64	Bold Faith	151
65	Declarations of Faith	154
66	Peace, Despite...	156
67	Lessons from Nature	159
68	Extraordinary You	162
69	Impressed by Jesus	164
70	Orphan Mentality	167
71	God is Faithful	169
72	Running the Race	172
73	Risky Living	174
74	Freedom and Contentment	176
75	The Real Battle	178
76	Community Has Power	180
77	Expectations of Church?	182
78	Closer Than We Realize	185
79	Death	187

80	Fathers	189
81	Money	191
82	Pursuing	194
83	Caring for Others	197
84	Loving the Difficult People	200
85	Peace	202
86	Overcoming Anxiety	204
87	Into the Unknown	206
88	Finishing Well	209
89	Step Out	211
90	Discovering Treasure	213
91	Sunshine	215
92	Meals	217
93	Our Father	220
94	You Could be the Next Dancing Dog	222
95	Spiritual Battle	225
96	Underestimating Small	228
97	The Professor and the Sandbox	231
98	I Now Realize	233
99	After the Silence	236

Acknowledgments

Writing is solitary for much of the time, but it is a team that publishes.

Thank you to Kyle for sharing the dream and encouraging the first compilation and helping shape the content. Deep appreciation and gratitude to Julie Frederick my copyeditor for her amazing attention to detail and expertise in smoothing my rather rough edges. Thanks to the team at Wipf & Stock for their expertise to make this book a reality. And of course, much gratitude and love to my wife, Vi, for support and encouragement to complete this project.

Introduction

It has taken about fifteen years to compile these musings. They first emerged in the form of a weekly email to members of the church I pastored as a means of encouragement and community building. Some are from my blog (johncoxauthor.ca). My underlying passion has always been to invite questions and to experience Christianity as relevant and real in our ordinary, everyday lives and relationships.

Most of the people I have met who want to follow Jesus are seldom satisfied with their progress. Like me, they have ups and downs in their journey, one day finding it easier to believe than on another day. These musings are for them.

The musings are arranged randomly and can be read in any order. You may stumble upon one written in the Christmas season, and it is June. I believe God will speak to us in a wide variety of ways, and a Christmas theme can resonate any day of the year. Each musing ends with a few thoughts to help us consider and apply what we have read, and a passage from the Bible.

Approach the exercise of reading these musings with expectation and take time to ponder and reflect—there is no rush to finish. You could spend a few days on one musing, reading the chapter around the Scripture quoted. You could randomly open the book and read whatever comes up. Don't be afraid to be playful with God; he is serious about our coming to him as children—curious, eager, with open hearts and minds. He desires to speak and encourage us more than we know.

Do you ever worry, or have anxiety about something? If, like me, you answer "yes," then you will know how to meditate. We're just more familiar with mulling over the negative. How about reflecting on the side of encouragement and hope for a while? It is my prayer that this book will help you to do so.

These musings cover a wide range of topics and are intended to provoke thinking and encourage venturing beyond small boxes of interpretation. If you don't agree with something, that's fine. Move on to the next musing, or better still, chat to a friend about what is bothering you.

May God take these very humble and imperfect words and use them to inspire you, to bless you, and to encourage you in your journey with Jesus, and through your daily life in a challenging, puzzling, and imperfect world.

1 | Burnt Toast and Marmalade

I love burnt toast. Scrape the worst parts off, add a little marmalade, and what was ruined becomes a treat to savor. Life can be like that with God. When times are hard or circumstances don't turn out as we'd hoped, with some patience and creativity new possibilities emerge.

In the moments when all we see is smoke and blackened toast—the defiled remnant of what had once been fresh bread in our hungry hands—what then? The burnt toast could be shattered dreams, the death of a loved one, career failure, a broken relationship, sudden injury, faith on life support. So many reasons to question and wonder where the hope is, and what is the way forward. How can we regain the passion to believe after this?

My life has touched those places of heat and smoke and smoldering dreams. Only an extra pair of hands much larger than mine has enabled a transformation from cremation to resurrection. It has been a journey of plummeting into steep valleys, then soaring to exhilarating heights with a stomach full of butterflies, the fog of apprehension pierced with bursts of sunlight. Life's a roller coaster!

Sometimes, when we talk about believing in God, an image pops up of someone sitting in a random church listening, and listening, and listening. "Where's the connection to my life outside of this religious bubble?" we might whisper.

Throughout the pages of the Bible, God meets people and walks alongside them in every conceivable venue. They converse by the ocean, alongside rivers, on top of mountains, in homes, up trees, in caves, in boats, in chariots, in fire, in thunderstorms, in earthquakes, in deserts, in vineyards, in churches and synagogues, in dreams, in visions, in books.

These encounters between God and his people invariably are interruptions—surprises—and usually unexpected events that happen while the person is on their way to somewhere else—or, perhaps, going nowhere.

CONSIDER:

Is God in a box in your head, restricted to speaking or working in specific ways and times? What if he's bigger and more creative? Listen for him in a new way today. How does God speak? He always begins with our name, affirming his love. He never speaks to us accusingly. He embraces us with his genuine acceptance, not necessarily of every attitude or behavior. From that place of acceptance, he gently reveals anything negative in a manner that helps rather than humiliates. He can speak in a whisper of a thought, through written or spoken words, through a picture, a fleeting impression, whatever way is most normal and intuitive for us, because he knows us intimately. Don't try hard to listen; just believe he is speaking, and you will hear.

John 10:27
"My sheep listen to my voice; I know them, and they follow me."

*Love will find a way;
indifference will find an excuse.*
Ukrainian Proverb

2 | Ashes into Gemstones

Jesus spent day after day with his disciples, walking along roads, teaching, healing—surprising those he met with a love and an acceptance they never expected. He lived with an authority, power, and self-assurance that was quite remarkable considering the political circumstances into which he was born. His home country was occupied by the Roman superpower of the day; his family was ordinary "working class." His opportunities for "self-fulfillment"—for instance, getting rich, or attending university—were zero. Add to that the fact that he was promised a significant spiritual ministry and had to wait thirty years before he was permitted to do anything publicly! How did he do it? After all, he was fully human, the same as you and I.

Yet circumstances did not appear to dictate his path. Instead, he embraced his life and situation without flinching or complaining. He seemed to be aware of another reality and truth underpinning the visible. That was the place of truth from which he derived his meaning, purpose, and sustenance—a trusting relationship with his/our Father.

Perhaps that's one of the reasons why Jesus came to earth in the first place: to broaden our horizons and to help us see truth beyond what we taste, touch, and feel every day, in other words, beyond the "natural."

To use an analogy from the previous musing, the trick or truth is never in the burnt toast. Rather, it is discovered within the heart and mind of the one holding the charred remains. I place my hands clutching blackened bread into the hands of the living God and remain there with patience—that's the key. I should not be surprised to find diamonds and glittering emeralds emerging between my fingers from among the crumbs.

That's what he does! Water into wine, stormy seas into tranquil waters, sickness into healing, death into life, enemies into friends, despair into hope. Dejection into direction, lost into found, drought into rain, aimless into purpose, barren into fruitful. Sometimes we try so hard and think the solutions are always rooted in us, or the blame, or the disappointment. Remember, there's mystery in this life. If we think all of life is without hardship—all fresh bread without even a burnt edge—then we will miss out on what God is doing beneath the surface; how he is turning the ugly parts of our lives into beauty.

As you read these words today, there's a high probability that either you, or someone you know, is experiencing burnt toast. There's no shame in that; we're not alone. But it's not the end.

CONSIDER:

Scrape off the charred bits (forgive, be forgiven, accept, embrace, yield), talk to God your Father—and trust him to turn the ashes into gemstones, the sadness into joy (or at least something more constructive to build upon)! Believe, be patient, be expectant.

ISAIAH 61:3

. . . and provide for those who grieve in Zion—to bestow on them a crown of beauty instead of ashes, the oil of joy instead of mourning, and a garment of praise instead of a spirit of despair.

3 | Fear Not

WHAT IF YOU WERE kissed by the frog of your nightmares only to discover the Prince Charming of your dreams standing at the doorway to heaven? And what if he knelt at your feet and the shoe in his hand fitted you perfectly? As you arose in bewilderment, you were transformed into who you were always meant to be. Your Cinderella persona fell away in the presence of such unexpected love and affirmation, revealing an heir to the throne—what then?

Many people speak about God or a "higher power" as if he were an ugly toad, croaking in the dark. An irritant more than a blessing, best kept at a safe and respectful distance.

Remember Robinson Crusoe—shipwrecked on a remote island, finding a single footprint on the beach, realizing that he was not quite as alone as he'd supposed? The realization of another presence on his island caused panic to rise as his imagination ran wild. Rather than being excited about company, and someone with whom he could share his adventure, he imagined an enemy to threaten his existence.

One day a footprint appeared in the dusty earth of Bethlehem and audaciously challenged our assumptions and preconceptions. Jesus Christ embedded his mark on the earth—God's footprint in the form of a historical person. Our initial response to Jesus may sometimes not be dissimilar to that of Mr. Crusoe stumbling upon a footprint on his secluded, sandy beach.

With this footprint we are forced to contemplate the unthinkable—that maybe we're part of someone else's picture. Of course, God realized that we Crusoes would be somewhat startled and alarmed by the revelation. Therefore, when he alerted others (Mary, Joseph, the shepherds) to the pending historic visitation of his Son, Jesus, his messengers offered words of comfort and reassurance: "Be not afraid."

Being afraid is a common experience when we first encounter God. Press through fear when it rises, because God is reaching out as a friend who likes you and desires to keep you company throughout your life. His motives are good and kind—to help and support rather than judge, hurt, or accuse.

CONSIDER:

Are you struggling to fit God into your picture? Or are you living as part of his bigger picture, confident in his faithfulness? Embrace the mystery of your present circumstances, trusting him to be with you. Be assured; God never causes negative things to happen to discipline, punish, or teach us lessons. But like every loving father, he gives us the freedom to choose, and allows things to happen that he does not necessarily desire. We live in a broken world with lots of poor choices and negative consequences intertwining and impacting others—often unfairly. What God does desire is to help you overcome and redeem what is negative. Do not be afraid. He is with you, for you, and will never leave you.

ROMANS 5:3–5

Not only so, but we also glory in our sufferings, because we know that suffering produces perseverance; perseverance, character; and character, hope. And hope does not put us to shame, because God's love has been poured out into our hearts through the Holy Spirit, who has been given to us.

4 | Time

TIME'S A FUNNY THING. Sometimes it is delicate and flits like a butterfly from day to day with lightness and joy. Then there are seasons where time is more akin to a dinosaur wading through mud—thick, heavy, and slow. I prefer the lighter version, but, as is the case with all of us, I have no control over time.

In the biblical accounts of people with famous lives and great spiritual pedigrees, the backdrop of time is easily ignored or missed. Yet, as the famous saying goes, "Time changes for no man." Consider how often the process of time was considerable between significant events in the lives of these individuals.

Cast your mind back to Moses, raised in an Egyptian palace where he lived for nearly forty years before he emerged from obscurity after killing an Egyptian in anger. He fled in fear and tended sheep and goats in a remote desert wasteland for another forty years. There is a whole bunch of time tied up there—moments when he must have fallen into despair trying to understand the point and purpose of his life. When God finally spoke to him through a burning bush, Moses undoubtedly freaked out (I sure would!). He used every excuse he could think of to wriggle out of the mandate to free his people from slavery. He loved the prayer for freedom, but the pathway required him to face the fear from which he had fled so many years ago. Often the very thing we long for in our fantasies terrifies us when the reality hits the ground at out feet. Then time stands still.

Forty days can be a drag. Forty months is an eternity. But forty *years*? That is nothing when we consider Jesus, born in a stable to be the long-awaited Messiah, the revelation of God on earth, the coming of the Kingdom, the Savior of the world. He was hidden, living with a peasant family in Nazareth, for thirty years. What does the Son of God do in Nazareth for that period? Your guess is as good as mine.

What can we do with our time on earth? Tend to what is at hand, care for those in our lives, and celebrate the goodness of God during the ordinary.

Often we want a frenetic pace of great experiences, overcoming, revelations, breakthroughs, and meaningful moments. When they seem lost in a drought of the ordinary, we wonder where God is. But life is made up of seasons of sprints and marathons, of growth and stagnation.

He is right by my side. Invariably, it is my misguided sense of "what should be" that prevents me from embracing my present. Perhaps it is not a drought, but merely an essential part of a life process—a season. Not everything is a blaze of glory and a firework event. Stillness, quietness, and calm anticipation amid the mundane can be food for the soul and a cradle in which a magnificent future is nurtured and weaned. Nothing is never happening.

During our marathon seasons, our winters, God does not forget us, or lose the plot, or withdraw his love or presence. In a finite world of clocks measuring seconds, minutes, and hours, sometimes time must pass for the fulness of God to be disclosed. The good news is that God multitasks and has many "fulnesses" to reveal.

CONSIDER:

There is no bottle big enough to capture the time that God has in mind for you and me. He wants us to have the time of our lives. What are we waiting for if all he has is ours *right now*? Assume he is present in you as you read these words. God is working with you to prepare you to live out your answered prayers.

Ecclesiastes 3:1–8

There is a time for everything, and a season for every activity under the heavens: a time to be born and a time to die, a time to plant and a time to uproot, a time to kill and a time to heal, a time to tear down and a time to build, a time to weep and a time to laugh, a time to mourn and a time to dance, a time to scatter stones and a time to gather them, a time to embrace and a time to refrain from embracing, a time to search and a time to give up, a time to keep and a time to throw away, a time to tear and a time to mend, a time to be silent and a time to speak, a time to love and a time to hate, a time for war and a time for peace.

5 | It's Unbelievable

THE MOST COMPELLING ASPECT of being a disciple of Jesus is that so much is hard to comprehend. I mean, Christmas, Easter, healing, life after death, God with us now?

Our *response* to something is more important than the something.

"How can this be?" we cry (the same question Mary asked). Whether it is the fall of Jericho, the defeat of Goliath, the birth of Jesus, the miracles, the resurrection, the transformation of the disciples, the conversion of Saul . . . we can go on and on.

For those we read about in the Bible who experienced God, they had to risk walking to the edge of their traditional thinking in faith *before* the Red Sea miracle in their present parted. They had to trust the character of God and his faithfulness, even in circumstances where everything within them wanted to protest and run back to the safety of their natural paradigms and parameters. We might reflect on these miracles and wish we'd been there to see for ourselves. It is easy to forget the trials and questioning that preceded the miracle.

The good news is that God is the same—yesterday, today, and forever. He is more than capable of demonstrating his presence and power in every age. While we cannot return to earlier times, he continues to be active, alive, and present today to provide the same support, breakthrough, and thrill . . . if we are up for it!

When we reflect on our opportunities and challenges, we can be overwhelmed or amazed. We choose to be amazed as we anticipate the future God has for us, even though at times it seems unbelievable and we cannot figure it out. We want to prepare for "the more that is to come" by appreciating the present. We desire our responses to be filled with faith and vision because we know who God is, and what he can accomplish.

It is rather like preparing the house and table for guests—much is done before they arrive.

How do we do that?

We remind ourselves often of the unbelievable God revealed in Jesus. Anything is possible with him. Instead of being overwhelmed and intimidated by our circumstances, we will be comforted and assured that God is greater than whatever we face. He is with us. Let us ask him to open our hearts, our eyes, our ears, and our faith to discern what he is saying. How is he leading us as we journey into our respective futures together? That is what the disciples faced when they endured the crucifixion and burial of Jesus. The resurrection was beyond their wildest dreams—unexpected and breaking out of every boundary of thought.

CONSIDER:

Your test today will be your testimony tomorrow. How could you reframe a present challenge into something more constructive? Or embrace a process rather than avoid, procrastinate, blame, or fight? How could God use this to grow, mature, stretch, and enlarge your capacity for making a difference? You might ask, "How will this be since I am . . . ?" Acknowledge your fears, weaknesses, struggles, and doubts. Give them over to God without shame or apology. Receive his courage, his strength, his peace, and his assurance as he reminds you of his faithfulness amid it all.

Luke 5:8–10

When Simon Peter saw this, he fell at Jesus' knees and said, "Go away from me, Lord; I am a sinful man!" For he and all his companions were astonished at the catch of fish they had taken, and so were James and John, the sons of Zebedee, Simon's partners.

6 | Easter—Every Day

Easter continues. The stone is rolled away, and the grave is no longer victorious wherever the Kingdom of God is proclaimed. Jesus is risen from the dead and there are witnesses. Heaven touches the earth and life will never be the same again.

It is hard for us to believe the truth of those words, isn't it? They can be momentarily inspiring, but how does that impact our lives today? Let us begin with a declaration—that with encouragement and a willingness to combat passivity, the walls will fall around areas that we never dreamed could be breached or defeated.

Easter is not just an awesome historical event. It blows open the door for the Risen Lord Jesus to pour out the power and presence of the Holy Spirit over all people, everywhere, all the time. Good heavens, that means you and me today!

In Acts, the early church began to discover the truth of this remarkable new beginning as they met together, every day (Acts 2:46). They experienced, firsthand, the wonders and miraculous signs, and many were added to their number. The same thing is happening today all over the world. There is no reason why God should be absent or defeated in our homes, our families, our neighbourhoods, or our personal situations. What looks grave to us is an opportunity for him.

One of the most effective ways to discover *more of God* is to confess to him your doubts and unbelief. He does not mind at all. As you're honest and authentic before him, thank him that he hears you and understands your struggle. Then press in, come closer, and see what happens. Give him something to work with.

Pray for the release of God's Spirit upon you and your circumstances. Not because you deserve it, but because you are hungry, needy, sick, and desperate. If you are tired of hoping or being prayed for—come closer. If you are nervous about the supernatural and slightly uncomfortable—come closer. If you are hungry and thirsty for more—come closer. If you want to be counted among those who will put aside everything, including busyness, to break through and know God alive, in you like never before—come closer. He invites us to ask, to seek, and to knock, and he promises to respond!

If you don't feel like it, or have other matters to attend to, postpone them for another time and come closer. Come to give as well as to receive. Let's give the Lord at least a portion of the time and energy we grant to medicine and the medical profession as we seek cures and release for our mental or physical illnesses, addictions, and problems. Of course, we can pray, "Lord, help me in my unbelief."

Then pull out the stretchers, break open the roof, shove through the crowd, reach out, and touch. That gravestone of a door will open for you as it did for Jesus, the disciples, Lazarus, and many, many others just like you and me down through the ages.

CONSIDER:

What is it that you would really like to ask, or talk to Jesus about today? No hiding or censoring to make a good impression, just honesty and transparency. Speak up. See what happens over the next week. Be prepared to receive a response, even if it's not in the way you might have expected.

MARK 10:51

"What do you want me to do for you?" Jesus asked him. The blind man said, "Rabbi, I want to see."

7 | Changing and Never Changing

All over the world harvests and celebrations take place year after year, embedded in the uncomplicated rhythm of the seasons coming and going, as unchanging as a metronome. It's their reliability—the utter predictability of winter, spring, summer, fall—that provide the backdrop, perhaps even the foundation, of our lives on earth. It is their constancy that allows us to plan the rotation of crops, the way we live, what we wear, how we prepare for the future, and much more.

People of every nation gather in some form to give thanks; to thank God for his provision and for the enormous privilege of having enough to eat and drink and share with others. I've seen very poor people in Africa and India expressing heartfelt gratitude even for the little they have. It is humbling. We thank him that when we plant seeds they grow, that the rain falls, the sun shines, the earth is fertile, and in the course of time the fruit and vegetables ripen. It is wonderful.

The predictability of the seasons is not the whole story when it comes to the Almighty. Perhaps he merely takes care of the basics to reveal a far more adventurous and unpredictable side to his character. While he faithfully nurtures plants and animals through the seasons, when relating with human beings he changes his approach. He refuses to treat us as inanimate objects or living creatures at the same level of life as a pumpkin or a lion cub.

When it comes to you and me, God invites us into a relationship where he is Father, and we are his beloved children. That is the perspective within which he operates, the backdrop of the Kingdom of Heaven against which all else is planted and harvested.

It's called the love of the Father—one season embracing all seasons that never changes. His love and faithfulness are ever constant, even as the seasons of our lives change. When our circumstances are cold and uninviting like winter, his love is constant and faithful. When times are fun and carefree like summer days, his love is constant and faithful. When we are filled with hope and expectancy like springtime, his love is constant and faithful. And when life is grey and disappointing like the withering in autumn, his love is constant and faithful.

When God breaks through and touches our lives and hearts it can be very unpredictable and turn our world upside down. Consider Abraham leaving his home country not knowing where he was going and then later being asked to offer his son Isaac as a sacrifice. Or Saul being confronted with the reality of Jesus on the Damascus Road and his miraculous conversion. Or Mary and Joseph's wedding plans being overturned at the announcement of Mary's unexpected pregnancy. Or the disciples constantly finding themselves out of their depth when faced with praying for healing, stormy weather, or violence. While the seasons and our circumstances change, the character and faithfulness of the Creator remains constant, unwavering, rock solid. His promise is to never leave us or forsake us, and he cannot lie. Being assured of that reality to help and support us in every season is the rock upon which we can stand, to know a strength that is greater than anything we might encounter.

CONSIDER:

If God's presence is with you—right now, irrespective of the season—does that make any difference? Remember how Jesus stood outside Jerusalem and said, "How I longed that you would come to me . . . " Perhaps he has more for you today than you realize. Thank him for his presence and provision, and you will receive.

DEUTERONOMY 31:6

"Be strong and courageous. Do not be afraid or terrified because of them, for the Lord your God goes with you; he will never leave you nor forsake you."

8 | Disillusionment

"The longer you stay in one place, the greater your chances of disillusionment."

—Al Spander, Journalist

So, how disillusioned are you these days?

Are you bright-eyed with wonder, alert and excited with expectancy, intrigued by God and what he wants to do in you and through you? Have you learned that God invites us into his life and purposes, not the other way around?

Or are you a little jaded, like the two friends walking on the Emmaus Road after Jesus has died, saying, "We had hoped?" Life seldom follows the preferred script for more than a few hours. Some of us are experiencing various challenges that we would prefer would go away as soon as possible. Be encouraged to welcome the presence of God the Father into those places; be strengthened through the process rather than crushed by the circumstances.

One of the most confusing aspects of life is the seeming randomness of how things happen and the inequitable distribution of wealth, rewards, and penalties. If we scan history, we do not have to look far to speculate how Third World countries have been exploited in the past centuries to feed the economic growth of the First World.

We are all aware of how the rewards reaped by the sports and entertainment stars of this world are ridiculously out of proportion to those who work in sweatshops or endure fourteen-hour days to put food on the table. A 2015 United Nations study researched personal wealth around the world: $2,200 income per adult places a household in the top 50 percent of the world's wealthiest; $61,000 income positions you among the richest 10 percent of adults in the world. More than $500,000 places those who qualify among the richest 1 percent in the world. Half the world, nearly 3 billion people, lives on less than $2 a day. The three or four richest people in the world have more money than the poorest forty-eight nations combined.

Disillusionment is the boundary between my expectations and God's truth. It is a "middle-earth" located somewhere between our limited perspective and God's perfect vision. We are gradually learning that God is always kind, never changes, and is unwaveringly *for us*, never against. When disillusionment kicks in, it is helpful to take a step back and perhaps ask God what we have missed along the way.

CONSIDER:

Are you disappointed or disillusioned today? Jesus walks alongside—tell him about it. Then listen.

LUKE 24:19–21

"About Jesus of Nazareth," they replied. "He was a prophet, powerful in word and deed before God and all the people. The chief priests and our rulers handed him over to be sentenced to death, and they crucified him; but we had hoped that he was the one who was going to redeem Israel. And what is more, it is the third day since all this took place."

9 | Reality Check

Spiritual disillusionment, having second thoughts, doubting, is as normal and healthy as a child growing out of their clothes during the process of maturing. It is a natural and inevitable consequence of being alive on earth; of having the freedom to think and feel, decide, choose, take actions, and even make mistakes. If we are never prepared to be wrong, then disillusionment will be our enemy and denial will be the friend that sticks closer than a brother. However, if we anticipate meeting disillusionment along the path of our life journey, it can be an opportunity for learning, reflecting, and proactively adjusting and changing in our quest for greater wisdom and maturity.

It is probably true to say that most of our disillusionment with God is born from perceiving him as far less kind, loving, and compassionate than he is. Paul knew all about such a predicament from his own life experience. He distorted God into a rulebook and a harsh dictatorial Pharisee—that is, until God tripped him up on the Damascus Road and turned his world upside down. There are many paths to disillusionment; what one brushes aside causes another to stumble and fall.

On the other side of his revelation, it was a vastly different Paul who spent the rest of his life teaching, explaining, and living out the Christian faith throughout the Middle East. Approaching his death by execution as his reward for being an active and influential Christian leader, he wrote from prison to believers in Ephesus:

> *I pray that you, being rooted and established in love, may have power, together with all the saints, to grasp how wide and long and high and deep is the love of Christ, and to know this love that surpasses knowledge—that you may be filled to the measure of all the fullness of God. (Ephesians 3:17-19)*

Why would Paul pray that the Ephesians would know God's love—that they would be rooted in it, and so filled to overflowing that when others bumped into them God's gracious love would spill out over them? I suspect one reason is that Paul had learned that the moment of disillusionment is a reality check, when what is authentically within us spills out. The truth most deeply rooted within us becomes manifest in the knee-jerk responses we give to life as we encounter it in all its various shapes and flavors. It is a moment of truth when our imperfections and flaws tend to be most exposed, and what and whom we believe in becomes obvious. Then we either default into self-preservation and self-defence, or we allow God to meet us and lead us more deeply into his love and strength that changes us first.

Unlike contemporary love that feeds off feelings, sentiment, and self-gratification, God's love is tough. It is not scared to bleed (suffering for good, like the disciples endured floggings), and sometimes intentionally bypassing feelings. Our only hope is that Jesus continues to be willing to be born again into the grubby stables of our lives and work miracles in our hearts and minds.

We are learning to dispense with disillusionment and reframe those moments, now viewing life as a vast array of paradoxes and mysteries. It is here we find the hope inherent in Christianity: a king is born in a stable, God suffers on a cross, in weakness there is strength, the meek shall inherit the earth. It is so irrational that it appeals to us and resonates in our spirits as typical of a loving, creative, and highly personable, just, and original God.

CONSIDER:

Talk to God about areas of disillusionment or disappointment. Listen for his response and perspective. Nothing is over yet! If we read only half of Paul's life, we would never get the larger picture—of how God used him way beyond his limitations and suffering. This can encourage us not to give up on our own journey and life story. There are chapters still to write that may well astound us. God is not finished with you, or me.

EPHESIANS 3:17–19

And I pray that you, being rooted and established in love, may have power, together with all the Lord's holy people, to grasp how wide and long and high and deep is the love of Christ, and to know this love that surpasses knowledge—that you may be filled to the measure of all the fullness of God.

A frog in a well does not know the great sea.

Chinese Proverb

---

10 | Passion

Way down south—at the tip of Africa where I was born—the atmosphere bounced to the rhythm of soccer balls, and elongated trumpets (vuvuzelas) filled the stadiums with the sound of wild swarming bees. The World Cup was underway, and across the globe people were tuning in day and night to follow the fortunes of their favorite team.

The outpouring of enthusiasm and passion is commonplace in hockey arenas, baseball stadiums, political rallies, rock concerts, and perhaps even local school presentations. Most of us love the excitement of participating in something bigger than ourselves.

Could these illustrations be an encouragement to ask the Lord for the same—and more—in our lives and gatherings?

Passion, enthusiasm, interest, fascination—in something, whatever it may be—evokes a hunger and thirst to repeat that activity. To spend more time, invest more money, travel to where others have more knowledge and skill that we could learn from. This might be in the pursuit of sport, work, cars, gardening, quilting, or whatever. There is nothing wrong with that. But how about God?

Here are a few reasons why I want to serve God, follow him, praise him, work for him, live for him, and perhaps even die for him.

He showed me the truth of who I had become without God. He looked for me. When he found me, he embraced me. Despite my awkwardness, he showed me his wounds, his cross, and my name written in his blood for the forgiveness of my rebellion and sin. He enabled me to believe in myself, and he invited me to discover life with him. He placed his Spirit in me and filled me from the inside. Nothing compares or satisfies as deeply as the integrity, purpose, and meaning with which he imbues my life. He lavishes me with the love of his Father. That love filled a void I had always carried around in my orphan spirit.

Passion, passion, passion, passion, passion, passion, passion.

When I rebelled, fell away, and wandered lost? He was the one who never let me go—never ever! He never gossiped, pointed a finger, or stabbed me in the back. He drew me to him, bathed my wounds, surrounded me with friends, provided for my needs, restored to me all that had been lost—and more. No one else comes close to what he has provided. His faithfulness, his delight in me, his promise over me for my future, his provision for the present. Truth is, I would probably be dead without him. I'm beyond grateful.

We will never know his amazing grace until we acknowledge our amazing disgrace.

Surrender, and see what God can do when all we have is placed in his hands. There's not one soccer player participating in the World Cup who learned his/her skills sitting in the bleachers watching others, reading a book, or even downloading soccer tips. They turned up for practices, for coaching, for matches, for one another. In such a proactive process, their "gifting" was honed within the context of a team, and even the inevitable battering and bruising of drills. If we passively wait . . . it will be a long and sad sojourn.

CONSIDER:

Ask questions, battle doubt, probe for reasons to believe. Expect, and trust God your Father to bless the opportunity you are giving him to work in you. Decide to participate and be authentic. Sing the songs, raise your voice, declare who God is for others to hear. Shout his praise at least as loudly as a soccer crowd; come to play not watch—and see what happens. Build relationships with others, do something different. And if you are already doing all of that, then keep going.

COLOSSIANS 2:1–3

I want you to know how hard I am contending for you and for those at Laodicea, and for all who have not met me personally. My goal is that they may be encouraged in heart and united in love, so that they may have the full riches of complete understanding, in order that they may know the mystery of God, namely, Christ, in whom are hidden all the treasures of wisdom and knowledge.

11 | Imagine

Imagine that you are brutally killed in front of your friends. Your friends would be horrified and traumatized by the grotesque cruelty and suffering they witnessed. Then, three days later, you miraculously rise from the dead and appear to more than five hundred people over the course of six weeks. You reassure them that your identity as God's one and only Son is indeed undoubtedly true.

Imagine you tell them with a broad grin that the purpose of your life, death, and resurrection is to make all you have, and all you are, available to anyone who seeks it. To offer them the power and presence of the Holy Spirit—the one who reveals the Kingdom of Heaven and the relational love of God the Father on earth! Imagine you give them a high five and encourage them to "go do it in my name. Heal, release, resurrect, proclaim, restore, rejuvenate, bring glory to the Father. Be united, forgive, show grace and mercy . . . go do it! Be empowered and accompanied by the Holy Spirit."

You are so excited at the prospect of what could happen when the wonderful and mighty power is released; when your best friend, the indescribable Holy Spirit, is poured into your friends on earth. It is as if hydrogen has been made available to fill empty balloons for the first time in history. How high they would fly? The prospects are mind-boggling. The power released to help them fulfil their dreams, and yours for them, cannot be exaggerated.

Then, imagine a few hundred years later looking over your shoulder. Almost no balloons are in the air. Nothing is visible above the horizon.

Imagine your despair as you lean in closer and discover that most of those who claim to be following you are arguing and bickering over the meaning of hydrogen. Some who believe are hovering inches above the ground clasping meager handfuls of balloons, their heads barely brushing the troposphere let alone the heavens.

Imagine your sadness when you discover that the longest annual celebration these people hold lasts for forty days as they remember your suffering and death. "Oh my God," you cry. "Why are they constantly weeping at my cross, instead of entering into the life it leads to? It should be the other way around—one day at the cross and forty days celebrating."

But of course, you, Jesus, have imagined all these scenarios, no surprises. You continue to patiently reach out to your people, encouraging us to enter into all that you have given; more than we can ask, imagine, understand, or ever make sense of.

CONSIDER:

My prayer is that we will never be satisfied with where we are, or what we know today in our relationship and experience with Jesus. We can choose not to be discontented with our limitations, but curious and expectant for new insight and revelation. We have captured only a fleeting glimpse of the limitless possibilities Jesus offers us. There is so much more! As our faith grows, we can soar to new heights.

ISAIAH 43:18–19

"Forget the former things, do not dwell on the past. See, I am doing a new thing! Now it springs up; do you not perceive it? I'm making a way in the wilderness and streams in the wasteland."

12 | God—in Human Form

MARS HILL IS AN OUTCROP of rock near the Acropolis where Paul addressed the great scholars, debaters, and philosophers of Athens. He could not fail to notice the various statues and shrines honoring the many gods they proclaimed to believe in.

It was the shrine dedicated to the "unknown god" that caught his attention. All within hearing would have known about it. Paul spoke boldly about the identity of this unknown god. He told the Athenians that this God became known in the person of Jesus. He lived as a man in Israel, died, and miraculously rose from death to authenticate his identity as the only Son of the living God.

The person of Jesus was a radical revelation of God. He emerged from the abstract and vague in the form of a specific human being at a recorded moment in human history. God became "Someone" in order that we could understand something of who he is and what he is like. It is unbelievable when we think about it, which makes it even more credible. In other words, if God is true and real then we can expect our minds to be stretched and for many aspects to be beyond our grasp. We need help to believe.

In the person and personality of Jesus we discover most clearly the nature of God. God's heart is love, his identity is Father, and his desire is for relationship and communication. He is kind and quick to forgive. Best of all, Jesus came to show us the way to enter a specific and concrete relationship with God—on earth. Because of Jesus God can be known, experienced; he is no longer vague or abstract. How, you ask? Well, that is what these humble musings attempt to ponder.

Because Jesus was made of flesh and bone like we are; because he entered the world in the same way as we did—as a baby—God can relate to us. He is distinct from the pantheon of Greek gods and goddesses familiar to the Athenians who wielded their power from a distant mountain, who tricked people by adopting various guises (think of Zeus and his many forms). God is not separate from us; he is one of us. He can be seen (in Jesus), he can be heard, he can be felt, and he can be questioned.

Why is this important for us today? Firstly, because we are encouraged to know God through Jesus and be enriched from the history and the personal encounters we read about in the Bible. Secondly, because it tells us that God is not vague. His greatest priority is a reconciled relationship with us. He created us to be socially connected (through Jesus not social media).

This helps us to appreciate why Jesus gathered around him people to keep him company on his journey. Why Paul spoke so highly of individuals forming "the church." Both illustrate the value of followers of Jesus being in community. Paul even talks about Christians being members of "one body" and warns them not to devalue one another: "The eye cannot say to the hand, 'I don't need you'" (1 Corinthians 12:21).

Many years ago God wrapped me over the knuckles because of my attitude. I was frustrated with church.

"If you had a bad infection in your foot, what would you do?" he asked.

"I'd take care of it and do everything possible for it to be healed," I replied.

"Why would you care?" he asked.

"Because it's the only right foot I have," I replied.

"Well, that's how I feel about relationships in my church. You give up and walk away too easily."

CONSIDER:

Just as it was important for God to demonstrate his word through the person of Jesus, so too he wants each of us to demonstrate his love and reality to those we live among. Sometimes that is a challenge—and that is precisely when how we conduct ourselves matters the most. Am I avoiding or walking away from something or someone God is drawing me toward? Do I need to understand why, or can I trust him with the outcome and do my best to be obedient, even when sacrifice (not martyrdom) may be involved?

JOHN 1:1

In the beginning was the Word, and the Word was with God, and the Word was God.

13 | What Now?

"Joseph, what do we do now?"

"Dunno to be honest, Mary. Carry on as normal?"

The teenage parents lay side by side on straw beside the crude feeding trough where their newborn slept. It was a few days since the shepherds had visited. Silence filled the night as Bethlehem slowly emptied of pilgrims. The light of the oil lamp cast shadows across the stable, its dim glow strong enough to keep thick darkness at bay.

"Sometimes I think it's all been a dream," confided Mary. "Hard to believe on so many levels. I don't feel very different—other than being a new mother, which takes my breath away. And you, Joseph, have been the most patient and understanding of husbands. Where would I be without you?"

Joseph sighed and pulled Mary closer. "Life with you has certainly not been dull." Mary turned her head in time to catch the smile play across his stubbled face and she grinned. Then her brow furrowed.

"But what now?" She repeated the unanswered question.

"Still clueless." Joseph shrugged. "I guess we follow the customs and take our baby to the temple in two days' time and then make our way home. If we're not deluded or dreaming, then it's up to God to answer that question. He did it for me once before when you insisted there was no other guy. Remember? One day at a time."

There were to be year-loads of ordinary in the extraordinary lives of Mary and Joseph as they parented Jesus. Like fellow Jews of the time, they would participate in the normal family traditions and festivals: annual journeys to Jerusalem, attendance at synagogue, family chores, earning a living. Even knowing that Jesus was a very special child, Mary and Joseph seemed to accept this rhythm, this mundane reality, rather than stress about what lay in store for them. Their attitude is totally in line with the God whom Jesus revealed as an adult—a God who has no favorites but embraces the everyday in all its beauty and ugliness; a God who offers his mystery, compassion, kindness, comfort, and strength to "others just like us" in a broken and often difficult world.

And if we listen, every now and then we might catch a word of encouragement, or a surprise affirmation that God indeed has his eyes and hands upon us. This is what happened when the freshly minted new parents took their son to the temple, not on the first visit, but on the second. On the first visit (as was the custom) Jesus was circumcised like every other Jewish boy—no bells or whistles, no angelic appearance or anything out of the ordinary.

On the fortieth day after the birth of Jesus, Joseph and Mary returned to the temple to present their firstborn as outlined in Exodus (13:12–16), as a sign of God's redemption when he brought the Hebrew slaves out of Egypt.

Joseph and Mary probably had no great expectations, no agenda; they were merely fulfilling the requirements of their Jewish faith and tradition. And there, amid the corruption, the religious ritual, the misuse of coins and sacrifice, God placed salt and light in the persons of Simeon and Anna. Who would have thought?

As they wandered through the enormous, probably rather intimidating temple, cradling their baby, they surely must have been puzzled. *Are we doing the right thing? Have we imagined this whole crazy idea of our son being chosen by God?* There had been no great outpouring of resources. They were poor rural peasants.

They had scarcely completed their meager sacrificial offering of two turtle doves when an elderly arthritic man approached, face beaming, arms outstretched. Joy radiated from his wrinkled face, his kind eyes glinting with mystical recognition, and his words wrapped them in affirmation, straight from heaven. "Yes, at last!" Simeon exclaimed. "I have waited so many years for this moment." He reached out and cradled the baby, holding him close to his chest so his beard tickled the child who grasped curiously at the long grey wisps. Simeon praised God, words tumbling like a waterfall over the child, splashing the wide-eyed mother and her husband. "My eyes have seen your salvation, which you have prepared in the sight of all the nations..." Tears streamed down the old man's cheeks when he finally fell silent and kissed the young Messiah on his forehead.

Then he grew somber as he returned the baby to his mother. Simeon looked at Mary, then at Joseph, then back to Mary. "This child is destined to cause the falling and rising of many in Israel, and to be a sign that will be spoken against, so that the thoughts of many hearts will be revealed. And a sword will pierce your own soul too."

Mary gazed deep into the old man's eyes as his words sunk into her heart. She felt the same presence as when the angel had appeared nearly a year ago announcing that she would be pregnant, a virgin with child. There was a flash of fear but mostly a surprising sense of peace and resolve that rose within her. She was only too aware that this child she held to her bosom would bring her great joy and unimaginable anguish. She nodded silently. She lowered her eyes as Simeon placed both hands on her shoulders and blessed her.

Joseph whispered, "I guess we weren't dreaming."

They were about to turn and leave the temple when another elderly woman appeared at Simeon's side. He nodded with a smile. "This is Anna. She has been here even longer than I have."

Anna shook her head when Mary offered for her to take Jesus. "No, my dear, I don't trust myself not to drop him." She chuckled as she placed her quivering hand gently on his head and addressed the crowd that had gathered around them. After offering more words of thanks, Anna spoke of how this child was the answer they had been waiting for, the redemption of Jerusalem.

Mary had tears in her eyes as she and Joseph left the temple. "Thank you, Lord," she whispered, "for giving us a word of affirmation and encouragement. I have no idea what lies ahead but I trust you. Thank you."

And so it is with us. We find ourselves surrounded by the unknown, among so much fear and confusion. God is perhaps silent even though many purport to speak in his name. We find it hard to see the extraordinary in the ordinary. What now?

CONSIDER:

The story of Mary and Joseph can be an encouragement to us. When you don't know what to do, continue doing what you know to be right and good. Keep up the traditions, and yes, even the rituals. God will bring each of us to Simeon and Anna in due course. The words from heaven may be a fleeting thought, a conversation, a dream, a song, a sense of peace, a book, a text or email out of the blue. You may be a Simeon or Anna for someone else when you least expect it.

JOHN 1:11–13,16

... to those who believed in his name, he gave the right to become children of God—children born not of natural descent, nor of human decision or a husbands will, but born of God ... Out of his fullness we have all received grace in place of grace already given.

The path is made by walking.
AFRICAN PROVERB

14 | Encouragement

"He was a good man, full of the Holy Spirit and faith, and a great number of people were brought to the Lord."
—Acts 11:24

I would love Luke's words describing Barnabas to be my epitaph; how about you? Barnabas is one of those characters so easily overlooked in the pages of the Bible. It is the qualities of people like him that are foundational to the strength and integrity of the wider Christian community.

Wooden roof beams, which are integral supports to a building's structure, are built by gluing (laminating) small strips together. The glue is hidden. The individual pieces of wood could never accomplish what the greater whole can support when firmly bound together. In this analogy, Barnabas (filled with the Holy Spirit) is the glue. He is remembered for his great encouragement and generosity.

In the days of the early church, people were learning that faith in God involves the visible expression of care and generosity to those around them. We read that the first Christians were extremely aware of one another's needs and ensured that no one went without. They shared all things. One of the first to model a light touch with money and a generous heart was Barnabas. He sold land he owned and brought the money and laid it at the feet of the apostles in Jerusalem to support their ministry (Acts 4:37).

Barnabas was not only generous; he was also courageous and discerning. It was Barnabas who introduced Saul to the suspicious and scared disciples in Jerusalem and vouched for the integrity of his conversion. Later he would travel to Tarsus and encourage Paul to share a ministry journey with him, resulting in the epistles (letters) that would form a substantial portion of our New Testament. Paul received the acclaim, while Barnabas remained in the background. I like to think that in his own modest way, Barnabas was applauding him and sending more checks whenever he could.

It is tempting to look for quick fixes or shortcuts in the Christian life. I know because I have tried. I get impatient and act impulsively rather than wait for clarity; ask God to bless something when I'm neglecting my responsibility or not putting in the work required. The reality is that there is no substitute for relationships forming the context of growth. Love is the key to releasing the meaning and power contained in every word of Scripture.

CONSIDER:

Let us not underestimate the power of encouragement and affirmation—of cheering on our friends and family from the sidelines. When we appreciate something, or have been blessed by someone, make a call, send an email, tell them face to face. Do not assume that person does not need the kind word. Try not to delay your affirmation or allow shyness to have the victory.

May you and I live like Barnabas today, rather than wait to express appreciation in epitaphs carved on cold stones. May we be like those roof beams, bound together by love and supporting one another. As best we can, let us encourage others, placing them and their success above our own, just like Barnabas enjoyed the gifts and success of Paul and was glad to be a part of it.

Sometimes we can discern gifts and potential in others who cannot grasp it for themselves. They need a friend to blow on the embers and help to ignite the Spirit within them that they cannot yet see.

ACTS 11:25–26

Then Barnabas went to Tarsus to look for Saul, and when he found him, he brought him to Antioch. So for a whole year Barnabas and Saul met with the church and taught great numbers of people. The disciples were called Christians first at Antioch.

15 | Freedom

I REMEMBER ONE EVENING in Paris drooling through a restaurant window at a juicy cut of lamb roasting on a rotisserie. I would have loved to order a meal but could not afford any luxuries whatsoever on my shoestring budget.

Much later in my life, when all was dark and silent inside me, I remember looking out at the world. It was as if all the streetlights had been turned off and I was left fumbling aimlessly, hopelessly, in the wilderness. Unlike the brightly lit Parisian streets, my inside place was a cave of wounded refuge. I had no desire to venture out. Instead, anger festered, eroding my soul. Irritability scurried around in the darkness like a pack of hungry rats.

Have you ever felt like this—seeing the world through paned glass, longing for what seems unattainable? Or feeling trapped inside yourself, looking out with equal helplessness? You are not alone. So many of us have felt locked out or trapped. Who can set us free, who has the keys?

Jesus is the only one I know who responds to both realities with astounding generosity and unparalleled love. He draws alongside all who appear to be missing out on the banquet provided for every citizen of his Kingdom and invites them in for a seat at his table. When we are imprisoned inside, he walks through walls and offers to kill rejection and unbelief, releasing hope and light into overwhelming darkness. At the same time, he never excludes anyone who wants in. He steps out to meet those on the outside looking in—yes, sinners like you and me—and invites them warmly to enter.

Jesus is life! He speaks truth with an open heart, out of which flows no condemnation or religious babbling. I could write pages describing how he has loved me into increasingly greater freedom, while at the same time helping me see how much is still to be conquered. I passionately desire to ensure that no one is abandoned in the streets, only seeing God's love from a distance and not entering the banquet he has prepared for everyone. I want to boast of the power of Jesus who broke out of a cave in the resurrection. He delights to enter our dark and hidden places to bring light, love, hope, and encouragement. And the wonderful truth is he never judges or condemns; we have already done that to ourselves.

I believe that to boast about Jesus and share his supernatural power is our commission and mandate. The harvest is abundant, the laborers are few.

CONSIDER:

Pray for many to emerge from the quicksand of apathy and become involved in harvesting on a consistent basis. Many hands make light shine. Here I am Lord, free me, use me—TODAY! By the way, it is friendship and kindness that will draw people to Jesus, much more than debates, accusations, and judgment.

Mathew 9:37–38
"The harvest is plentiful, but the workers are few. Ask the Lord of the harvest, therefore, to send out workers into his harvest field."

Don't ask God to guide your footsteps if you are not willing to move your feet.
Portuguese Proverb

16 | Organic Church

THE WORD "ORGANIC" IS very trendy these days. Supermarkets sell fruit, vegetables, and other foodstuffs labeled as "organic," meaning it's been grown without the use of pesticides or other chemicals. In a way, our farming methods have come full circle and we have gone back to basics, not wanting any additional, potentially harmful "extras" added to the food we eat. And so it is with church. The idea of "Organic Church" is rooted in going back to the central message of Christianity, of rediscovering the raw honesty and relational integrity of the first Easter. The crucifixion was the furthest thing from anyone's mind when the disciples daydreamed of their future with Jesus. Like us, they could probably only faintly see beyond the immediate horizon, focusing on day-to-day tasks rather than the bigger picture. It was only much later they realized that Jesus was part of a greater plan to bring salvation to the whole world and change human history. His agenda extended far beyond living, dying, and rising again for a few lucky chosen people in Jerusalem and Galilee two thousand years ago.

The radical revelation of the cross is that God takes our sin, disobedience, and rebellion very, very seriously—because it creates an unbridgeable chasm between us and him. It is not a response of anger toward us. It is anger toward the cause of the rebellion— satan (I never write his name with a capital letter), whose power was broken on the cross.

If you've ever lived anywhere with bears, you've probably heard the advice never to get between a mother bear and her cubs; a bear's love is fierce, and she will protect her cubs no matter what. That is what God is like, why Jesus came to this earth, and why he went to the cross. Passionate love for his offspring led him there. It mattered that much. It demanded that degree of radical intervention, sacrifice, and showdown with the political authorities and religious leaders of the day. It was a rescue mission through and through.

Organic Christianity is passionate, personal, edgy, challenging, painful, sacrificial, exhilarating (nothing beats resurrection). It impacts life close to home with friends and neighbors. It gets people talking. It overflows with goodness and kindness.

It is about ordinary people encountering an extraordinary God through the transformed lives of people like you and me.

Organic Christianity is about a refreshing transparency in relationships. It's about quitting the religious "BS" and pretense of perfection. Mistakes are embraced amid space to learn, repent, and grow. There is a commitment to authenticity, because it is much less stressful and far more exciting, though seldom convenient.

On the first Easter morning the disciples ran to Jesus' tomb. They returned with news that it was empty. Those they told accused them of talking nonsense. Some wept in confusion and wandered around the garden, aimlessly questioning events . . . until the real risen Jesus opened their eyes—and they believed the unbelievable. They didn't pretend to believe or understand when they had no idea. Their authenticity with God and with each other was the foundation of their radically changed lives.

That is what Organic Church is meant to be about—people gathering around the unbelievable news of Jesus as honestly as possible, learning together how to step into the revolution of the resurrection as it impacts their lives. Organic Church has no time for prima donnas or egotistical leaders who demand applause, or those who try to laud it over others. Why? Because growth is a lifelong process, not something that can be achieved in a moment. We are all works in progress—never complete—and we need to be upfront about that or we risk stagnating.

It is that level of truthfulness that we are learning to love. Because unless we understand our predicament, we will never revel in the glorious gift of grace released through the cross and the resurrection. We cannot have "grace like silk" without the harsh "disgrace" texture of the cross, mingled with sin's blood and nails.

Organic Church is not about a leadership team, or a worship group, or anything other than a community desiring to live out what it means to be a disciple of Jesus filled with his Spirit. Truth means proclaiming the goodness of God, the favor in his heart to his beloved, the joy he offers, the healing that is found in his Kingdom, and the "always more to come." As God's children, we must care enough to encourage one another and graciously challenge one another.

Organic Christianity is always astounded and amazed by what God is doing, fostering an insatiable curiosity about what he desires to accomplish among us. It is about delighting in worship, spending time together in his presence, and caring for the lost, the sick, the wounded, and the lonely.

CONSIDER:

Can you be real and authentic with those around you? Less than perfect? Are you a safe place for another to reveal their incompleteness, doubts, and sins? Can you be transparent about your weaknesses while accepting that those around you are also a work in progress?

JOHN 8:1–11

At dawn he appeared again in the temple courts, where all the people gathered around him, and he sat down to teach them. The teachers of the law and the Pharisees brought in a woman caught in adultery. They made her stand before the group and said to Jesus, "Teacher, this woman was caught in the act of adultery. In the Law Moses commanded us to stone such women. Now what do you say?" They were using this question as a trap, in order to have a basis for accusing him. But Jesus bent down and started to write on the ground with his finger. When they kept on questioning him, he straightened up and said to them, "Let any one of you who is without sin be the first to throw a stone at her." Again he stooped down and wrote on the ground. At this, those who heard began to go away one at a time, the older ones first, until only Jesus was left, with the woman still standing there. Jesus straightened up and asked her, "Woman, where are they? Has no one condemned you?"

"No one, sir," she said.

"Then neither do I condemn you," Jesus declared. "Go now and leave your life of sin."

17 | No Doubt About It

Mind reading, second-guessing, and believing the worst are tendencies most of us appear to be quite skilled at. Negativity and doubt about ourselves, how others see us, and our faults and weaknesses—these loom large in our psyche. In some cases, this is called the "imposter syndrome." *I'm not as good/skilled/clever as everyone thinks. When people find out the truth, they will expose me as the fraud I really am. Will they still follow me? Will I keep my job? Will I retain my power and my prestige?* These are thoughts typical of one who feels like an imposter, a fake.

I know this might sound exaggerated, but it is not far from truth. And what makes matters worse is that we live in a climate of hypocrisy, judgment, and cruel vindictiveness fueled by a puritanical sensitivity and political correctness. No living creature can survive the laser-like public scrutiny that lays out one's entire life under a microscope to find any evidence of inconsistency, wrongdoing, or even a crumb of fallibility. How ridiculous, heartbreaking, and far adrift we are from the grace, mercy, and love of God.

I remember long ago standing in the schoolyard while two popular boys were picking sides for a game of tag rugby. Those who wanted to play stood in front of them as they took turns to select their team. Obviously, the best athletes were selected first. But what stung most was the humiliation of having my name called last. As the runt, I shuffled over to a team, unwanted, the words "Guess we're stuck with you" echoing in my head ever since.

Many of us feel like that when we consider standing before God—as an inept, fallible runt at the end of the line who's not worthy of being picked at all. So why bother?

That is such a lie!

The good news is that God, whose character Jesus revealed with such dignity, kindness, and courage, is not like what we have become at all. He chooses every one of us to be part of his team.

He says that the weak will be first, the last will get to the front, and the imperfect and broken will be at the head of his table. He never posts pictures of our failures on Instagram to highlight the flaws. If anything, he scans our hearts and minds to call up the potential and the hidden giftings. He finds the treasures that have been lost and forgotten amid the pile of disappointment or discouragement that life often brings.

Consider this. A middle-aged man turned up at the *Antiques Roadshow* in England with a small, decorated box enameled in gaudy yellow with some poorly drawn figures on the lid. The inside was somewhat damaged. "I found it in the bottom of a box at a boot sale, bought it for 20p," he told the appraiser. After a long description, the appraiser told him it was made for royalty, was hundreds of years old, and valued around £20,000. "Amazing find. Only in England can you still find such treasures," he exclaimed to the owner who was utterly flabbergasted.

Twisted negative thinking has inundated church and Christian teaching. Take, for example, the theology of predestination. A wide spectrum of Christian thinking believes that only some are chosen by God, with the rest destined for the fires of hell. The idea originates in the words of Paul about those whom God has chosen: "For those God foreknew he also predestined to be conformed to the image of his Son, that he might be the firstborn among many brothers and sisters" (Romans 8:29).

It is an interpretation reflecting our fractured thinking rather than the heart of God. No wonder so many want nothing to do with those who profess belief in God. But what if predestination declares that the living God chooses *all*, loves *all*, and has predestined *every one of us* to know him and embrace his invitation and revelation of love? The fact that some will not accept the invitation rests on personal choices and responses, which in themselves hold much mystery.

How we think is important. It makes a world of difference to begin with a declaration that you are chosen by God. You are his first choice, not the runt. What if we began with that affirmation as we approach God, with no doubt about his love, his goodness, his delight in us? Here is an earlier verse in Paul's letter to the Romans: "But God demonstrates his own love for us in this: While we were still sinners, Christ died for us" (Romans 5:8).

The key is understanding that God took the initiative, not only in creation, but also in redeeming. He searches for you and me because he regards us as much-loved children, not junk. He is neither disillusioned nor alarmed by our failures and secret sins. He knows all about them and merely acknowledges them as symptoms of how we are hurting and trying to compensate for what we do not realize he has to give us.

CONSIDER:

If you are feeling discouraged, disqualified, wounded by the judgments and accusations of others—take heart. Expose the lies and turn again to hear the words of the Father affirming his love. There is hope for you today and in the future, precisely because he is fiercely passionate to see you found, healed, and restored. You are made for royalty. He wants to lift you up and have a party in your honor, not just when you first come home, but many times along the way. Smile, God loves you!

Ephesians 1:3–6

Praise be to the God and Father of our Lord Jesus Christ, who has blessed us in the heavenly realms with every spiritual blessing in Christ. For he chose us in him before the creation of the world to be holy and blameless in his sight. In love he predestined us for adoption to sonship through Jesus Christ, in accordance with his pleasure and will to the praise of his glorious grace, which he has freely given us in the One he loves.

18 | Dead and Alive

Remember the great Western movies with posters reading, "Wanted—Dead or Alive," above the picture of the villain being hunted down? Churches often resort to that approach: whether you are dead or alive, please come, we will not make you feel uncomfortable. The emphasis has been on attendance numbers rather than encountering the living God.

The poster should read, "Wanted—Dead and Alive!"

Paul wrote in his letter to the Romans that followers of Jesus should "count yourselves dead to sin and alive to God in Christ Jesus" (6:11). In other words, step into the gift Jesus provided on the cross. There he released forgiveness and grace for every act of rebellion that was out of line with God's will for us.

God has never had a problem with the reality of our sinfulness. He is neither disillusioned by it nor offended that we struggle with temptations. He sent his Son Jesus to take care of what is overwhelming for us and beyond our capacity to deal with. That is why the revelation of our sinfulness does not have to be depressing; it merely affirms our need for a Savior. Much like being caked in mud leads us to running water, soap, and a shower, our mistakes or uncleanness lead us to the cross. It is good news!

This does not imply a cavalier approach to sin or suggest that our rebellion does not matter.

"Count yourself dead and alive" proclaims that we are caked in mud, have utilized the gift of a shower (the cross, sacrifice, death, and resurrection of Jesus), and it is great to be clean. Furthermore, we have been given a key to access the shower of grace anytime. God the Father provides the use of his sin-cleaning/forgiving facility to all his children twenty-four hours a day.

The problem is that many people think being "clean" is the whole point of the story, as if all we need to do is camp around the doorway to the touchless cleaning center and drive through in the name of Jesus multiple times a day.

That would be as nonsensical as buying a car and parking outside the carwash, only using it to polish and clean every day, obsessing about not getting it dirty. No, Paul is saying "come alive" to God in Christ Jesus to roam out there in the big, wide, dirty world and show them what alive and clean looks like. "Where did you get so clean?" will be the question from others scratching mud-caked heads. What does clean look like? Not spotless, but friendly, kind, servant-hearted, humble, joyful, hopeful, encouraging . . . get the picture?

We can love Jesus and believe in God and the smile is not always beaming; every day does not necessarily radiate with hope or victory. Of course, it should—if we were perfect Christians. But we are not. What is far more compelling is living with authenticity and hope during the process of growing in maturity and confidence, as followers of Jesus.

CONSIDER:

We've touched on this before but it's a big deal worth repeating. How easily can you live with authenticity before others? In other words, share your weakness, be unafraid to fail while trying. Accepting yourself and others as they are is an ongoing process. Many of us find receiving a challenge. Can you truly receive God's forgiveness for all you have ever done that is wrong or that you regret? Can you allow Jesus to wash your feet and even allow others to support you, do things for you, be generous to you?

2 CORINTHIANS 12:9

But he said to me, "My grace is sufficient for you, for my power is made perfect in weakness." Therefore I will boast all the more gladly about my weaknesses, so that Christ's power may rest on me.

19 | TOGETHER WE THRIVE

HAVE YOU EVER MADE something you have been so proud of you could not wait to show someone? It could be your first drawing at school, or a project you completed—anything really. It could be a dance, a song, a restored engine, a flower arrangement. The act of sharing your creation with someone increases the pleasure of creating. I wonder where that tendency within us comes from?

I have a sneaking suspicion it has something to do with our DNA, how we are created. Within us we bear the image and DNA of our Creator. He, and we, are fundamentally social beings who thrive on interaction with others. It is why solitary confinement is such a terrible form of punishment for human beings. When we are isolated, we diminish and withdraw; we don't become more alive.

God had no sooner spoken creation into being than he created Adam to stroll through Eden with him. He formed Eve to keep Adam company because he said it was not good for Adam to be alone. Adam needed "someone with skin on" to share his life. Communing with God was not enough. It was God himself who designed and created that fundamental human trait and provided a solution.

Many centuries later, Jesus traversed the region of Galilee and called individuals to follow him. They became known as his disciples and followers. After the resurrection they gathered and shared possessions—many more joined their ranks. Later, when Peter and Paul traveled across Asia, they planted churches from Jerusalem to Corinth to Athens to Rome. The result was groups of Christians who met together to baptize new converts, break bread, support one another, heal the sick, and proclaim Jesus as Lord. Many would be persecuted and became martyrs. They died for their faith in Jesus under extreme conditions of torture and humiliation. The church never knew such an accelerated period of growth.

Christian brothers and sisters supported one another as they endured the hostile and cruel centuries under Roman occupation and rule. They were not perfect by any stretch of the imagination; there was in-fighting, false teaching, sexual misconduct, and more. The Bible does not cover up or excuse the negative; all was exposed when Paul wrote letters to bring teaching and correction where necessary. That is authenticity.

With the emergence of the Bible, we receive the teachings of Jesus and the letters Paul wrote to the early Christian church. Jesus talked about loving one another, identifying himself as the vine and likening his followers to branches that would be pruned to bear fruit. Paul described the church as a community, equating the individual members to various parts of the human body. Each needed the other for the whole to function well, even when those parts were quite different—an eye being nothing like a foot, for instance.

These are the foundations and core values of what it means to be Christian. It is why belonging to a church is important, not merely a matter of preference or an optional extra. Implicit in the teachings of Scripture is the affirmation that believers gathering is a hallmark of God's Spirit working in them. People who love to play hockey practice together; those who enjoy singing meet regularly. Those who follow Jesus are molded and formed in their faith as they build relationships together, with Jesus at the center. Isolated, we become stunted or spiritually deformed.

We are made for relationship.

CONSIDER:

Is there a challenge in many churches to build community as friends and followers of Jesus? What are some of the challenges people face when trying to create a community where all can thrive? Do we offer to participate, or do we passively wait for our needs to be met by others? Do we make it easy for imperfect people to be included in our community "warts and all"?

Genesis 2:18

The Lord God said, "It is not good for the man to be alone. I will make a helper suitable for him."

20 | JESUS MAKES A DIFFERENCE

WHEREVER JESUS WENT HE touched people (literally and figuratively), leaving many in his slipstream who had "come alive." They were eager to proclaim his impact on their lives, how they had experienced an unexpected awakening of hope and joy. It was a profound revelation to discover that God and joy were always intended to be the foundation of human life on earth. That the Father's heart is passionate for relationship.

I have taken much too long to take hold of this truth, run after it, and claim it as my own. I mistakenly interpreted my circumstances as indicators of my favor with God (or lack thereof). Consequently, I spent too much time struggling to survive—to be honest, often feeling passed by. I subsequently have learned what a lie I was subjecting myself to. How it eroded my relationship with God. It robbed me of joy. It often left me isolated and alone inside, while the outer mask portraying "everything's fine" kept slipping, despite my best efforts.

To encounter Jesus is to discover the wellspring of love and joy. When I was in Israel, I hiked down a deep riverbed called the Wadi Quilt. It winds through barren and rocky wilderness from the foothills of Jerusalem to Jericho. Along one side runs an aqueduct built by Herod to carry water down to his palace on the outskirts of Jericho. The temperature was about 120 degrees, and all the way I followed the aqueduct flowing with clear, refreshing water. I began the hike at the wellspring where the water bubbled up from underground as it has been doing for more than two thousand years.

The love and joy of God is like that . . . it never runs dry. But to access its refreshing qualities we must locate the source and then step into its flow. There is a lot of talk these days about staying hydrated—almost to the point that we do not leave home without our bottle! Imagine if we as Christians were hydrated with overflowing joy and hope irrespective of our circumstances. I don't mean being offensively trite and nauseating but exuding a confidence and peace, secure in the Father's love and his faithfulness.

Jesus prayed for his disciples, asking the Father that their joy would be full, not eked out in small measures to keep them alive on the way to heaven. Remember how he promised a never-ending supply of water to the woman who met him at the well? Much to her surprise, he also named some of her most carefully guarded secrets—for which she bore great shame—but did not reject or judge her. If you don't know the story, take time to read it in John's Gospel (Chapter 4).

I am praying for that kind of head-to-toe drenching in my life—not in a theoretical sense, but for real. I am inspired by the promises of Jesus pointing to an attainable experience on earth as it is in heaven—today. I am praying for churches to become wide and rich floodplains where many find nurture, hope, joy, and profound healing . . . in Jesus. The signs and wonders will be Christian men, women, and children dripping wet in a dry wilderness, unashamed to speak of what they have seen and heard, and more than willing to lead thirsty people to Jesus.

CONSIDER:

If you were drenched and filled by God's love and Spirit, what do you think you would look like? What do you desire more of? Perhaps he wants to release those things in you, and through you, and is doing it already. How about living from his acceptance, power, and affirmation—won for you and given freely to you, through Jesus?

2 CORINTHIANS 1:20–21

For no matter how many promises God has made, they are "Yes" in Christ. And so through him the "Amen" is spoken by us to the glory of God. Now it is God who makes both us and you stand firm in Christ. He anointed us . . .

21 | Praying

I AM PRAYING FOR young people to be inspired by relationships with adults who live out their faith authentically. Adults who have a passion for Jesus and who invite others to question, explore, and discover truth in their hearts for themselves. Adults who encourage them to invest in friendships of all ages where they can flourish and learn healthy self-awareness.

I am praying that all generations experience a powerful encounter with a relational Jesus who is relevant in their lives now; that they understand it has nothing to do with being "good enough" or spiritual, but is dependent on faith and expectancy. And that these encounters with Jesus will cause them to chase after more.

I am praying for God to continue to bless, encourage, and heal those who have recently entered a Christian church community. That it will be a safe and accepting place where everyone can discover hope and freedom, whatever their context or background. That they are courageous, honest about their need, and willing to do the work to see transformation. They are a wonderful gift whom it is an honor to welcome and walk alongside.

I am praying for a rise in passion for those who have been members of a church for a while. That their hearts will burn, and their joy will be a testimony of hope to others. That worship will be delightful, energetic, and buzzing with expectancy wherever people gather in his name. That each member will set the pace and not lag behind or be distracted.

I am praying for those who give time, effort, and resources to build and nurture their community church. That they may sustain, and even increase, their involvement and that their enthusiasm will draw others in to help. That, working together, they can build a house of hope, healing, power, and joy around Jesus. For sacrifice and generosity, acceptance and grace, to be the hallmarks of a Kingdom culture.

I am praying for a community who live for others. Who are generous because they have learned how to receive within their own lives and hearts; who are no longer afraid to give everything to Jesus. It is not, "This is for me, and this is for you." Instead, the mindset and heart response is, "Here I am Lord . . . it's all for you!"

I am praying that we can live from the inside out, with a faith that declares God's promises even before they have been experienced. And I'm thanking and praising Jesus for what he has already done, for the glimpses of "all of the above" that are evident, and for the promise of more to come.

CONSIDER:

What would happen if we switched our mindset from passively waiting to proactively stepping out, in the expectation that our lives could be fuller, richer, more joyful tomorrow than today? Jesus is Immanuel—"God with us"—yesterday, today, tomorrow. Now.

MATTHEW 15:31

The people were amazed when they saw the mute speaking, the crippled made well, the lame walking and the blind seeing. And they praised the God of Israel.

If you don't know where you're going, then any road will do.

TIBETAN PROVERB

22 | Not Much is More Than Enough

Years ago, I worked as a veterinary technician in the poorer townships around Cape Town. We would arrive at a designated area each week, open the truck equipped as a mobile clinic, and treat animals that were household pets. Skin conditions (mange), worms, distemper, and malnourishment were common ailments. Our arrival was a celebrated event and hordes of kids in the neighborhood would gather around us.

The children were always laughing and playing amid the dust and squalor. I witnessed their ingenuity and creativity as they fashioned racing cars from wire and bottle tops with long columns for steering wheels. With squeals of delight, they ran around driving and "racing" barefoot in the dirt. It seemed they could take anything and creatively fabricate something useful. In the process, they derived enormous pleasure and joy.

This picture has stuck with me as I have traveled in the more affluent regions of the world. By and large, while there has been an abundance of "stuff" everywhere, I have never found the same degree of creativity and infectious joy shared by those kids playing in the dust around the "doctor's truck." It's amazing what rises to the surface when we must make do. When it comes to creativity and innovation, it seems that less truly is more.

I have a sense that the same principle is true with God and the workings of his Kingdom. I wonder whether those of us who have grown up in or around church have not become dulled in our senses as to what could be?

Do we always need one more learning experience, one more course, a few more months, before we are ready to step out of the boat and do? Has the institutional church unwittingly spawned "needy" Christians who are comfortable within the safety of their church community, and who need those dependencies to protect them from implementing the very truths of which they speak? What if the Kingdom of God is not reliant upon our ability to "get it," or our expertise? More important, perhaps, is our willingness to allow God to work in us and through us in our weakness and incompleteness.

What would happen if we pressed the pause button on courses and conferences? If we encouraged one another to step out and invite the Holy Spirit to accomplish his work in us and through us—incomplete and imperfect as we are and always will be? Wasn't that truth exactly what confounded the religious leaders when Peter and the other disciples stood before them? Miracles had been witnessed through their speaking and touching. Their claim to fame was that they were unlearned and uneducated, but God used them anyway. "Not whom we would have used," the leaders muttered. But it was not the priests and officials who had made cripples walk and blind people see. Instead, they were preoccupied with rules and regulations.

Please don't think you're not good enough, don't know enough, or haven't got what it takes for God to work powerfully through you to bless others. All it takes is willingness. Tell him you are available and watch what happens.

Being authentic in our incompleteness with Jesus beside us is enough. You are enough. Imagine, if kids can make cars from wire and bottle tops, what God can do with your life, gifts, and circumstances right now. Not tomorrow, not in a few months' time, not only when the sun shines.

CONSIDER:

Treasure emerges in the most unexpected places when the hands of a mighty and creative God and Father are free to move. Ask God to open your eyes to see what you may have missed right in front of you.

ACTS 4:13

When they saw the courage of Peter and John and realized that they were unschooled, ordinary men, they were astonished and they took note that these men had been with Jesus.

23 | Learning from Nature

Do you ever get exasperated with God, because so much of life seems to involve maintaining stuff and tidying up?

I mowed the lawn a few weeks ago. When I look out of the window today the weeds are bobbing their cheeky yellow faces in the breeze taunting me—again! I guess I'll fire up the engine and mow 'em down, but they'll reappear as sure as the sun will rise and the rain will fall. Their roots go so deep into the earth; it is unbelievable how hard it is to get rid of them!

Nature has a multitude of parables that apply to life. I do not always appreciate the fact that sometimes I must act if I want to see a better outcome. I am not thrilled with lawn-mowing, for instance. When I first started a garden, I prayed for God to protect it from the deer. Weeks went by and all was growing wonderfully. Then, one morning I discovered the heads of roses chewed off; all I had nurtured had been digested by the pesky four-legged invaders. There was nothing for it but to build a fence. Ever since then the deer have never been a problem.

From annoyingly resilient weeds, I learn that if my roots go deep, I can survive almost anything. And from the garden I soon discover that when neglected it does not take long before it is overgrown and untidy. If I leave metal outside, it rusts; over time paint peels after exposure to weather. Constantly begging God to make it different does not appear to be a request he responds to. In other words, God does not wave a magic wand to make life easier without any effort from us. In the same way, he does not mess around with the reliability of scientific principles, such as gravity, centrifugal forces, evaporation, and rainfall.

The visible is frequently a springboard into understanding the invisible and spiritual. It is no surprise that when it comes to the Kingdom of God and learning to live "from heaven to earth" similar principles apply.

Understanding the contrast between the two realms is fundamental. Life on earth without God is about ownership, possession, self-fulfilment, holding onto what you have, hoarding for the future, and basically relying upon your wits and will power. I do what I want and ask God to bless what I have chosen to do according to whatever my priorities happen to be.

In the Kingdom of God (living from heaven to earth), God is King. Citizens of his Kingdom are interested in fulfilling, discerning, and aligning themselves with his will. They have learned that his ways are different. The atmosphere of his realm is permeated with love, light, cooperation, and empowerment. They don't keep rules as much as live in a secure and affirming relationship with the Father—where doing his will is freedom and joy. They are not driven by having to earn his approval or have their identity determined by the perfection of their accomplishments. They are sons and daughters whose lives are fulfilled as they grow in sensitivity to his heart. They experience the peace that comes with being assured of his love, presence, and power every day. Sons and daughters, heirs of such a magnificent Kingdom, do not have to rely on themselves. They are constantly discovering that the resources available to them to live life "on earth as in heaven" are beyond what they ever imagined.

CONSIDER:

If you are a follower of Jesus, you are a member of his Kingdom. How does your citizenship in heaven impact your life on earth? Do you welcome the hands of the ultimate Gardener pruning and nurturing your life, even utilizing fences?

SONG OF SOLOMON 2:15

Catch for us the foxes, the little foxes that ruin the vineyards, our vineyards that are in bloom.

24 | Gardening and Fences

In the Bible vineyards often are used to describe life. Jesus talked about himself as the vine, and us as the branches. He said that we need to keep close to him to receive his love and power. A core principle for us to embrace is allowing his Father, the Master Gardener, to prune us from time to time—so that we become increasingly fruitful. In Song of Songs there is a warning to guard against the little foxes that will do damage in the vineyard if the owner does not pay attention. In other words, build fences and act. This will assure ongoing protection for the good things beginning to blossom.

The application that I am learning is that if I allow my life to "just happen" then I am ruled by anxiety, invariably poking through the fertile ground of circumstances that overwhelm. If I do not put safeguards in place (my fences), the foxes of old habits or thought patterns sneak in and cause havoc. I am learning to invest in the Kingdom of Heaven, my goldmine of resources and support. I am experiencing the truth of Jesus' words to seek first the Kingdom of God and then everything else will follow. How do I do that?

The fences are disciplines rooted in very ordinary human activities. I read the Bible every day, specifically to learn what this Kingdom looks like and what I can anticipate. The information is on every page. I need to be rooted in the truths I find there. I place a high priority on worship alone and in the presence of others (yes, there are many forms). That means opening my heart to the Lord and singing songs of praise to him, or dancing, painting, writing, being silent, and anything else you can think of as an offering. I ask and desire him to soften me and make me more tender than the "natural me" would ever be.

I am learning to abide and live from a place where I know God the Father loves me; he has made everything he owns available to me. He wants me to become good at relying upon him and experiencing his presence every day. I find that challenging because so much of me only sees and experiences the mundane world around me. I am learning there is more to reality than meets the eye.

I know that I am not able to do anything worthwhile for God in my own strength, so I am working on developing a stronger relationship with the Person of the Holy Spirit. He speaks through thoughts, feelings, other people, circumstances, and even symbols and dreams, helping me grow as a citizen of this unbelievable Kingdom. I am learning that believing does indeed lead to seeing. And that my mind and understanding usually lag in making sense of it all.

Another fence or building block for me is that I absolutely need others around me. Gathering for worship on Sundays is quite often not what I feel like doing. However, it is essential that I come before the Lord to seek his presence with others without an agenda. Often there are surprises, and I know that I am receiving more than I discern because of that obedience. I accept that some of these actions on my part will be challenged by foxes or involve having to say no to other possibilities and even needs. I have decided that it is worth the sacrifice to invest in the Kingdom of Heaven that is growing in me. I understand that it will not happen without my commitment and cooperation. In fact, when it is hard, I am learning to take pleasure in the challenge while demonstrating to God my serious intent. I love the truth that "fire falls on sacrifice."

Be encouraged. God wants the relationship *more* than we do. He will meet us *more* than halfway and will help us *more* than we realize.

CONSIDER:

How is your garden growing? Anything proactive that you can do to nurture the growth? How about declaring:

"I am encouraged to see buds and fruit emerging because of paying attention and deciding to reject passivity. I am hungrier than ever for God's Kingdom and am growing in confidence to take risks and trust his Spirit to be released. My expectation and faith are rising to anticipate evidence of God's Kingdom breaking through in church, to heal the sick and restore broken lives and hearts. I know more of his joy than ever before, and I hear him much more clearly in the pages of Scripture."

2 Timothy 1:12–14

That is why I am suffering as I am. Yet this is no cause for shame, because I know whom I have believed, and am convinced that he is able to guard what I have entrusted to him until that day.

What you heard from me, keep as the pattern of sound teaching, with faith and love in Christ Jesus. Guard the good deposit that was entrusted to you—guard it with the help of the Holy Spirit who lives in us.

There is no right way to do the wrong thing.

Turkish Proverb

25 | Thanksgiving

"Thanks be to God for his indescribable gift!" Paul wrote to the Corinthians (2 Corinthians 9:15). He was talking about Jesus and the grace God the Father had shown him when he (Saul/Paul) was walking in rebellion, in the opposite direction from God's purpose for his life. Paul had followed Jesus for many years by the time he wrote those words of thanksgiving and praise.

I always marvel at such enthusiasm and gratitude and continue to ask God to mold me into that quality of character as I grow older—being thankful as a lifestyle no matter what the circumstances. Thankful for God's faithfulness because he is always kind and good, even when the situation I am experiencing is not what I prefer.

I recall Jesus at the Last Supper with his friends, including one (Judas) who would commit the ultimate breach of friendship and betray him when he most needed support and encouragement. Jesus gave thanks for the bread and the wine set before them on the table. He transformed them into eternal symbols of his body broken on a cross and his blood shed for the forgiveness of sins. He gave thanks amid suffering, because he knew that if he endured, others would be blessed, rescued, set free, healed, and reconciled. Jesus, forever drawn into the love of his Father, empowered by the Spirit that filled him on earth as in heaven.

Paul left no stone unturned in his reflections upon Jesus and in his remarkable lifestyle. He never avoided the tough stuff while he proclaimed and lived in the victory that had already been won. He wrote to the Philippians that he regarded the accomplishments of his life as nothing in comparison to what he was experiencing in friendship with Jesus. He leaves us in no doubt of his passion when he exclaims, "I want to know Christ and the power of his resurrection . . . " I would have stopped there! Paul continues, "and participation in his sufferings" (Philippians 3:10).

Peter says the same thing in his first letter: "Dear friends, do not be surprised at the fiery ordeal that has come on you to test you, as though something strange were happening to you. But rejoice inasmuch as you participate in the sufferings of Christ, so that you may be overjoyed when his glory is revealed" (1 Peter 4:12–13).

These men were confident of the big picture. They knew with deep conviction that in the face of every death and moment of suffering there would come a resurrection. They lived with abandon, completely sold out to letting life unfold . . . the good, the bad, and the ugly. Whatever happened, they were joyfully convinced that God is good, he loves them, and he holds them close. If he could use their feeble lives to illustrate his faithfulness, they were more than thrilled.

But let us keep it real. Sometimes suffering is hard, particularly when it is impossible to find a good reason that could possibly align with God's will. Paul and Peter were not always upbeat. Sometimes they struggled with circumstances, lack of support, insecurity, peer pressure, disappointments, and everything else we all face from time to time. However, amid all of that they declared the truth rooted beyond themselves and their frailties.

Why this somber tone for thanksgiving? It is not really. In an age of nonstop entertainment and self-absorption, where faith and thankfulness tend to hinge on our personal happiness, comfort, and circumstances, we need reminding of where the source of all we are really lies. Thankfulness in the Promised Land is not the same as a turkey dinner in Egypt.

Slaves at the table are grateful for survival and the crumbs they receive. That is good, I suppose. But what about sons and daughters of the King who feast at his banqueting table in the Promised Land? They enjoy their inheritance, already served on earth as in heaven—hot, steaming, fresh, and delicious. They do not say grace as much as live in the generous light of his amazing grace. They drink, chew, and swallow in full view of their enemy because they know they are kept safe in Jesus.

CONSIDER:

Pull up a chair, tuck in, give thanks . . . you are invited to the feast. Try to reframe hard challenges or circumstances. Ask God for his presence and wisdom. Declare his faithfulness and goodness no matter what.

Philippians 3:10–14

I want to know Christ—yes, to know the power of his resurrection and participation in his sufferings, becoming like him in his death, and so, somehow, attaining to the resurrection from the dead.

Not that I have already obtained all this, or have already arrived at my goal, but I press on to take hold of that for which Christ Jesus took hold of me. Brothers and sisters, I do not consider myself yet to have taken hold of it. But one thing I do: Forgetting what is behind and straining toward what is ahead, I press on toward the goal to win the prize for which God has called me heavenward in Christ Jesus.

26 | Mindsets

"Easy to access and hard to leave!" For so long churches have been institutions with professional clergy as the gatekeepers—sometimes even self-appointed bodyguards keeping the public at a distance from God. Sounds rather silly really, but it is human nature to slide into control mode, gravitating toward rules and qualifications.

God's Kingdom is incredibly welcoming. It never requires status, wealth, or education as a prerequisite to entering. There is only one way into the Kingdom, and it is through Jesus. When he was crucified, rose from death, and released his Spirit, he provided the way in—for all who responded to his gift of forgiveness, reconciliation, and grace.

Learning and understanding grow as we mature in the Kingdom, on earth as in heaven; it is not required beforehand. That is why when Peter gave his first public address, three thousand were invited in through baptism that same day. Within a few hundred years the "official church" was demanding nine months of instruction. Religion began to stifle the fresh, invigorating wind of the Spirit.

Peter had a dream about his traditional Jewish roots forbidding him from eating "unclean food" with Gentiles. God's Spirit corrected him and instructed him to share the love of Jesus with non-Jews, the Gentiles. As God moved among the Gentiles, the leaders in Jerusalem had to change their deeply held mindsets that had never considered such a possibility until it actually happened. In Acts 15 they meet together and reflect on what God is doing. They conclude that "we should not make it difficult for the Gentiles who are turning to God" (verse 19).

In other words, they will not have to jump through a bunch of Jewish hoops before being accepted as fellow believers, and possibly even being used in ministry. Such an approach does not imply that nothing matters.

Rather, it recognizes that when people encounter the reality of God alive and confess Jesus as their Lord and Savior, then they are to be welcomed into the community as full members and citizens. Of course, teaching and growing in relationship with Jesus and one another will be encouraged as an essential ingredient to mature in the Christian faith. Importantly, knowledge and even wisdom are not prerequisites for identity, worth, or access to the Father.

God's desire is that we all become servant leaders who lay down our lives for others, share generously, and participate in doing the works of Jesus. It seems to me this is an exciting truth. The safeguards to protect the individual and the community are rooted in relationships rather than an adherence to rules (although there is a place for guidelines, values, etc.). Relationships in this instance imply openness and being teachable, humble, transparent, willing to be corrected, and even more willing to encourage and quickly forgive mistakes. It means asking for help. It means recognizing that each of us is a mixed bag of good, bad, and unresolved issues that God will be working on (and through) for the rest of our earthly lives.

CONSIDER:

How easily do you give up on others—or yourself—when things go wrong, mistakes are made, or nothing seems to change?

LUKE 23:42–43

Then he said, "Jesus, remember me when you come into your kingdom!"

Jesus answered him, "Truly I tell you, today you will be with me in paradise."

JOHN 14:1–3

"Do not let your hearts be troubled. You believe in God; believe also in me. My Father's house has many rooms; if that were not so, would I have told you that I am going there to prepare a place for you? And if I go and prepare a place for you, I will come back and take you to be with me that you also may be where I am."

27 | Stay with It

A FEW YEARS AGO, I went diving at the Great Barrier Reef in Australia. I had a card showing that I had completed the course to be a certified PADI diver. The only problem was that I had not participated in any diving for about seven years. Consequently, when I donned all my gear and jumped in, I panicked and had to resurface. With the help and encouragement of the instructor, I slowed down and descended to spend a total of eighty minutes exploring the Barrier Reef fifty feet underwater.

Upon reflection, I saw the parallel with the Christian life so clearly. It is one thing to carry the card of membership; it is quite another to be engaged and living the life. Imagine gathering a bunch of people together to play a new ball game you have invented. You call it some amazing name, hand over the ball, and tell them to go for it. You have vaguely explained what it is about, but before long confusion breaks out and frustration grows as they do not really know what to do. "Tell us the rules," they desperately ask, "so we can play properly."

We intuitively understand that rules in games provide structure that enables us to enjoy playing with freedom and passion. "Principles" sound better than rules, but whatever we call them, they are essential not just for games but for every aspect of life—what we eat, how we drive, how we travel, how we relate to one another . . . the list is endless. Therefore, it is no surprise that Christianity is the same, yet totally different.

One of the speakers at a conference I attended said, "The amazing thing is that some people believe that following Jesus and being Christian is actually possible—in our own strength." That comment illustrates a fundamental principle for those who follow Jesus. In our weakness is his strength; without him we can do nothing (John 15:5). It was not an accidental remark but highlights a core truth. Jesus was transparent when he declared that he only did what he saw his Father doing and that he could accomplish nothing by himself (John 5:30).

It is interesting that the most controversial aspects of following Jesus and listening to his teaching invariably cluster around the work of the Holy Spirit, the gifts of the Spirit, and the manifestation of signs and wonders. Coincidentally, they happen to be those aspects of Christianity that take us away from ourselves and invite us to yield and be less self-reliant, and entirely dependent upon, what he can do in us and through us.

I am convinced that God's Kingdom is about sharing and witnessing the extraordinary revelation and power of Jesus healing the sick and touching hearts through ordinary people filled with his presence today. The church is not a spiritual "good works" meeting on Sundays. It is a gathering of people who experience the love of the Father and see him working through them from Monday to Saturday. They congregate to worship him, encourage one another, and testify to his greatness on Sunday. We can no more do the works of the Kingdom without the Holy Spirit than we can remain underwater without an oxygen tank.

The only thing required is to jump in and learn to use the equipment, which is active learning rather than passive information-gathering in isolation. I am excited about what God is doing and what he will be releasing among us.

CONSIDER:

Are there places, relationships, or challenges where you are holding back for fear of making a mistake? I encourage you to participate, jump in, get wet, and do not give up at the first sign of fear or mystery! It is never too late to reactivate the Kingdom card!

JOHN 15:5

"I am the vine; you are the branches. If you remain in me and I in you, you will bear much fruit; apart from me you can do nothing."

28 | Dark Days

ONE OF THE HARDEST lessons I have ever had to learn was how to embrace the present when my days were black, the future was shrouded in fog, my legs were lead, and my heart was barely beating. Depression is indescribable to those on the outside.

To believe that depression will ever lift is unimaginable. I had to stop telling myself what I should or should not do, feel, think, or accomplish. Give myself permission to be where I was—one day at a time. But I still focused on circumstances and other people, complained about unfairness, and existed in a constant state of being overwhelmed by my past and present. Survival was what life had become. The road ahead was a total mystery to me as I concluded that nothing ever seemed to work out.

Linking all those thoughts into one muddled outlook left me alone, believing that even God had cast me aside. This was after many years of knowing Jesus. As circumstances overwhelmed me, my heart closed, my focus shifted, and I began to drown . . . and scream, "Help!"

The disciples did not magically follow Jesus with unquestioning devotion without struggle or moments of turmoil and even despair. Simon Peter experienced his share of being humbled as he darted from the exhilaration of walking on water to sheer terror when he thought about it and began sinking. He was as confused and out of his depth as the others were when Jesus suggested they find the resources to feed over five thousand hungry people. One day he was confident, promising to follow Jesus everywhere. The next he was scurrying like a coward into the darkness after denying he even knew Jesus. Humiliated, he retreated to his area of expertise—fishing—and caught nothing.

That is where Jesus met him—in his place of emptiness and broken resolve. This God whom Jesus was revealing was the real deal. He was one of a kind, faithful to the unfaithful, persistent in love, relentless in kindness, and not a bad breakfast chef either.

Another time, these tough fishermen/sailors/disciples were absolutely terrified on a lake in a storm. Jesus slept peacefully in the same boat. He had to get up and calm them and the storm, assuring them that he did care. "Calm down," he said. On another occasion, they were trying to obey his directive, example, and teaching, by praying "with authority" over an epileptic boy. Nothing happened. When Jesus appeared, the boy's father virtually mocked their efforts before Jesus effortlessly healed him. Jesus did not laugh at them for their failure. He encouraged them to keep trying and used the moment to take them further in their training and development.

Thomas decided to follow his own agenda after the crucifixion and allowed his skepticism to draw him away from the other disciples for a while. Consequently, he was AWOL when Jesus entered through the walls of the locked Upper Room where his friends were hiding in confusion and fear. Later, when Thomas heard what had happened, he was angry, hurt, self-pitying, and struggling to believe what the others were telling him. Jesus waited another week before making a personal appearance to Thomas and assuring him that he was not left out of the Father's embrace.

CONSIDER:

Everyday life is the context in which God works and where Jesus meets us. Christianity has nothing whatsoever to do with romantic idealism or spiritual dreamlands. The more authentic and hungrier we are to see him at work in our lives, the more we will experience. Prepare to be stretched. Where is he working in you today?

MATTHEW 14:25–31

Shortly before dawn Jesus went out to them, walking on the lake. When the disciples saw him walking on the lake, they were terrified. "It's a ghost," they said, and cried out in fear. But Jesus immediately said to them: "Take courage! It is I. Don't be afraid."

"Lord, if it's you," Peter replied, "tell me to come to you on the water."

"Come," he said.

Then Peter got down out of the boat, walked on the water and came toward Jesus. But when he saw the wind, he was afraid and, beginning to sink, cried out, "Lord, save me!" Immediately Jesus reached out his hand and caught him. "You of little faith," he said, "why did you doubt?"

Lower your voice and strengthen your argument.

LEBANESE PROVERB

---

29 | Beyond My Comfort Zone

UNCOMFORTABLE AT TIMES AND inconvenienced on occasions. You will not be able to wrap your mind around the living Jesus. There will be moments when you want to cut and run. If you have never experienced rising panic, or a rush of adrenalin in your pursuit of Jesus, you may want to ask yourself why that might be.

I remember fear to the point of paralysis when I had to stand up in front of people and speak. It began in my youth group as a teenager and persisted into my early thirties as I began full-time ministry. On one occasion I was totally embarrassed and flustered in a small group of people trying to "be free" and raise my hands in worship. But a few weeks later, that pathetic little crisis (a big deal for me) was honored by God, and he unlocked something in me related to freedom in worship that has never left. I had theological misgivings about the Holy Spirit and the terribly controversial speaking in tongues, battling for years with my insecurity and awkwardness.

A hippie, tent-making pastor laid hands on me in Cape Town when he discerned that I needed a nudge. I spluttered some sounds that could never have been God-induced—so I thought. A few days later, I knelt by my bed and made more sounds for twenty minutes and felt nothing, concluding that it could not have been God. Two years later and two thousand miles away, I knelt at my bedside again and tried this "useless gift" one more time to pray for my ailing grandmother. Within a week she had mercifully died, and I saw God smile.

That same pastor kindly agreed to speak at our small youth group one Friday evening. He gave a vibrant talk about Jesus being alive. I was horrified when he asked if any of the kids wanted to be filled with the Holy Spirit so that Jesus could be alive in them too—tonight! He expected something to happen after he talked! I will never forget the broad grin on

Phyllis's face as she experienced the presence of Jesus in her heart for the first time that evening and the excitement that followed. I will also never forget my tears and the wonder, walking home through dark streets. My pulse pounded inside as I asked Jesus to forgive me for my chicken-heart. I told him that I wanted to sign up and follow him for the rest of my life if he were as real as this!

Some years later, I had the opportunity to do what the pastor had done and pray for someone to be filled with God's Spirit so they could be alive with Jesus. But I was still too unbelieving that God could use me; I spluttered and stuttered my way through a nerve-wracking few days. The leader I was supposedly helping laid hands on me and smilingly asked God to use me anyway, then shoved me out into the arena. Amid my floundering, where all discernment left and I was totally disoriented, Jesus spoke to me through my thoughts. He encouraged me to let go of all the pressure and self-doubt; to just bring people to him and he would take care of the answers. I did. All of heaven opened, and the joy and excitement that welled up in me was worth more in my heart and spirit than years of books and classes. Other people were touched and experienced him alive when I prayed for them!

We are no different from those first disciples with our fears and misgivings, our tendencies to run away, our preference for comfort and wanting to have preeminent authority and control. Following Jesus is to encounter unconditional love and acceptance. It also can be the most exhilarating journey into wholeness. It involves taking risks, facing fear, showing humility, yielding control, being changed from the inside out, accepting inconvenience, stepping out on water, feeling inadequate, discovering your identity, being empty, being filled, being disappointed, being overjoyed and amazed; making sense of nothing, then having your heart and mind opened to see what you never could have comprehended or imagined to be true before.

It is about learning to trust Jesus in the everyday, humdrum world. A turning point for John Wimber years ago was when God spoke to him: "You've done ministry your way, now let's try my way!" Jesus continues to invite us along his road less traveled and take a few risks along the way.

CONSIDER:

What facet of Christianity are you most uncomfortable with? Why? What would help? Are you open to having your mind or attitude changed?

1 Corinthians 14:5

I would like every one of you to speak in tongues, but I would rather have you prophesy. The one who prophesies is greater than the one who speaks in tongues, unless someone interprets, so that the church may be edified.

The usefulness of a cup is in its emptiness.
Chinese Proverb

---

30 | Character

ONE OF THE MOST confusing things about following Jesus and understanding the Kingdom of God is learning that the way things work is often the opposite to how we naturally operate. For instance, in our culture, core values center around our accomplishments, whether we've achieved our personal goals, how successful we are. In the "natural" world, life is measured by achievements. We strive for recognition—play sports for grand prizes, win scholarships for good grades, and take satisfaction in the awards that have been bestowed upon us.

In the "supernatural" world—the Kingdom of God on earth and in heaven—what matters is our character. God looks at who we are, not so much at what we do. "Well done, good and faithful servant." His priority is developing character in disciples of Jesus. That is a process often overlooked, or that many would prefer to sidestep. Sometimes we volunteer for things and get frustrated when life does not turn out as we want it to, in terms of outcome or accomplishment. We complain to God. He must remind us that his focus is on who we are becoming in the process. We have one outcome in mind, and he has another.

A sign of maturity in our Christian growth is when we learn to submit to the process and yield control. We trust the Lord and ask him what he is teaching us as we intentionally make ourselves available and enter learning in the context of community.

We can get discouraged sometimes because nothing seems to be happening. Much of life can be mundane, punctuated by rare moments of fame or glory. If your life seems a little bland, instead of focusing on a desired outcome, begin to ask Jesus what he is teaching you in your present circumstances. Perhaps it's patience, or faith, perseverance, or humility, or . . . ?

CONSIDER:

Embrace whatever it is before you today as a gift from a Father who knows your needs and loves you with great generosity. Anticipate positive outcomes regardless of where you are. See what happens as he works in you and around you. Resist passivity; rather, step into the life he has for you. Enjoy now. Do not postpone contentment until everything works out or is perfect; you might be waiting a long time.

PHILIPPIANS 4:11–13

I am not saying this because I am in need, for I have learned to be content whatever the circumstances. I know what it is to be in need, and I know what it is to have plenty. I have learned the secret of being content in any and every situation, whether well fed or hungry, whether living in plenty or in want. I can do all this through him who gives me strength.

31 | On Fire

WE SPEND THE EVENING talking about all this power Jesus gives us, and his authority to overcome evil. We talk about being sons and daughters in God's amazing Kingdom. Astounding, even revolutionary—yet why isn't it more exciting? We talk about it, look at our watches, and say, "Time to go home."

We need a fire lit inside us. Where is the evidence of our faith and hope? Why do our prayers seem to go unanswered? Is power and victory only for a select few who are more spiritual than we are? Why is there so often a gap between what we read in the Bible and our everyday experience?

Our response is somewhat lukewarm much of the time, isn't it? There's no blazing fire; more like a flickering candle extinguished by the slightest breath. We are busy, disengaged, distracted. Our expectations are deeply impacted by our lives in a very fractured world. But it is the tragedies, the loss, and the suffering that Jesus came to earth to redeem. "Well, he seems to be losing the battle," the cynic retorts. When he hung on the cross they mocked, "You're the Son of God—command angels to rescue you." Not one flutter of an angel's wing was heard as Jesus bled, died, and was stabbed. Three days later, the tomb was empty, angels appeared, and the cross looked entirely different in the light of the resurrection.

God is completely unlike us in how he works. Left to myself, I see more of the negative and tend toward despair. I am not a natural optimist and can easily get down on myself and go quite dark (which is usually that spiritual orphan raring his head as a victim). Fortunately, God embraces me in my incompleteness wherever I am. When Jesus walks alongside me, he declares my identity as his beloved, his creation, one whom he knows and for whom he has a future that is fulfilling and wonderful. Everything changes when his perspective replaces mine. Hope fills me afresh. The promises of identity, purpose, authority, and power ignite a fire within me.

What I thought was impossible becomes possible, probable, and even actual over time. Jesus is the only one capable of lighting a fire within. I remember years ago hearing the analogy of logs and coals being piled on top of one another to form a blazing fire. Remove a piece of red-hot coal from the fire and it quickly cools. It is the gathering that keeps our individual fires burning. It is having God and Jesus in us and being aware and thankful for their presence; being part of a community that builds a fire. Isolation is the quickest way to grow cold and be overwhelmed by the environment and the negative voices in our head.

CONSIDER:

May the love of the Father and the power of his Spirit ignite such a fire in you. May your identity as his son or daughter be evident as his authority in you touches others and draws them to him. May this roaring fire of his love be warmth in you that can be shared—much more than words, opinions, or ideas of perfection.

The disciples were disillusioned and confused after Jesus' crucifixion. They asked the stranger walking beside them questions (Luke 24:13–35), and then the fire burned inside their hearts. What questions along the road on which you are walking do you have? Ask, discuss, pursue the answers. Fire will come.

LUKE 24:32

They asked each other, "Were not our hearts burning within us while he talked with us on the road and opened the Scriptures to us?"

32 | Plans

How is your life this week? On a scale of one to ten, what does it feel like to be you today?

Are you encouraged, optimistic, excited, fearful, lonely, overwhelmed, so-so, or something else? Do you have great plans or no plans? Are you still learning and growing, adventurous and willing to take risks? Or have you become discouraged, weary, and withdrawn to the point of having no expectations—to a place where it is hard to smile?

Wherever you are as you read this, and whatever your response, where is Jesus in the scheme of things? Is he making a difference? Or is that just another problem causing guilt, anger, or indifference to rise within you? What do you do with those questions deep within when answers are hard to come by?

I have found myself in such a place several times along my journey. One day it seemed all was unfolding beautifully, and then everything crumbled and I could not find reasons or God's hand. Often the toughest reality is realizing that following Jesus is a journey through many seasons. Disciples of Jesus fail, struggle, doubt, mess things up, and seldom have everything together, or definitive answers. Having safe relationships to share authentically helps us all as we journey together. Never be ashamed to struggle or to ask why.

The words that broke through my turmoil were the same as those whispered by the Father to the older brother in the prodigal son parable (Luke 15:11–32): "All I have is yours." Like piercing light breaking through dark clouds, God's Spirit embraced mine with a truth I had avoided or missed for so long . . . in my heart. It was, quite simply, the invitation to walk into the love of the Father and trust him with all that I am—once and for all. I was on the brink of bankruptcy, in emotional chaos, and confused about my purpose and future. When I finally yielded, the waters gradually parted and miracles of grace, provision, and purpose began to emerge.

I could give so many testimonies to illustrate that revelation over the course of my life, and in the Bible. Think about Jesus calling Simon Peter to follow him after he experienced a miraculous catch of fish. Jesus was teaching on the shore of Galilee and then stepped into Simon Peter's boat and asked him to take them a little way out to catch fish. It was a ridiculous request, as no one ever catches fish in the shallows of Galilee in the daytime. Simon Peter reluctantly agreed, threw the nets over the side, and they were filled with fish. Go figure! This was no abstraction; it was knowing the presence of Jesus in the place where he, Simon, was an expert. Supernatural authority was declared over the natural. Is that possible?

Jesus did it in his backyard. Simon Peter was absolutely stunned by the unexpected haul of fish! Jesus took the initiative and asked to enter Simon's world by borrowing his "stuff." Then he blessed him in a manner he never anticipated.

When Jesus issued the invitation to follow him, Simon was fired up inside. He said yes without hesitation. He saw it as an opportunity to pursue more of the truth and reality he had experienced in this remarkably unconventional man. This brings us back to where we started, when I asked how you are feeling about yourself, your life, and your future. Where is Jesus in that discussion?

The great news for those of us who are weary and heavy-laden is that he is offering to carry all that weighs us down—in exchange for our trust. For some of us that's wonderful news, particularly when it is accompanied with the promise that "All I have is yours." It is a generous exchange, trading rags for riches; purpose and hope replacing meaningless, tired survival; company and direction instead of being lonely, lost, and floundering.

What happened to Simon's plans that Jesus interrupted—plans for a fishing business, perhaps other projects, and aspirations around Capernaum? I guess they became insignificant and not nearly as exciting. In the Old Testament, God's people had plans that took them away from him in their rebellion, resulting in seventy years of captivity under the Babylonians. During that discouragement, God spoke through Jeremiah words of truth and promise: "I know the plans I have for you . . . plans to prosper you and not to harm you, plans to give you hope and a future" (Jeremiah 29:11). By the way, they were in captivity, and remained there for many years before this promise was fulfilled.

The adventure we are invited into with Jesus is to be so aligned with his heart that we participate in his plans, even if it means letting go of ours. That is the road to vibrant identity, belonging, peace, joy, and even signs and wonders as citizens of his Kingdom. Living out the meaning of his will being done on earth as in heaven . . . in me and through you today!

CONSIDER:

Talk to Jesus and try answering those questions posed at the beginning of this reflection. Simon Peter's common sense could have stopped him from obeying Jesus' request to go fishing. Does common sense sometimes get in the way of taking a step of faith? Remember "risk" is how faith is spelled.

JEREMIAH 29:11

"For I know the plans I have for you," declares the Lord, "plans to prosper you and not to harm you, plans to give you hope and a future."

33 | Investing

Robert Bateman is probably one of Canada's most famous wildlife artists and enjoys a worldwide reputation. Some love his work; others disregard it as too realistic—such is the world of art. I think his love for nature and his ability to capture it is amazing. On one occasion, I had the pleasure of hearing him speak about his life and career. He talked about his early years learning his craft while collecting specimens for museums, doing geological surveys, and eventually teaching. Every day he drew sketches and painted, and for years hung around artists and mentors, observing and interacting with them, and being open to their critique and inspiration. Eventually, while he was teaching in Nigeria, someone asked for more of his work and a career as a full-time artist began.

A young Irish fellow by the name of Rory McIlroy won the US Open in 2011 after four days of scintillating golf and a fair chunk of pressure. The story behind his rise to fame and success is an inspirational one of parental support and sacrifice—as well as hours, days, and years of practice, learning, application, competition, testing, and more practice. Rory's parents recognized an extraordinary talent in their only son. They did everything with their meager resources to help make it happen—for him to become the best he could be. You probably have your own examples of other sporting success stories or remarkable achievements.

How about the story of a fabulously wealthy and powerful person agreeing to his only son going in the totally opposite direction for the sake of others? Jesus laid down all that we would call success, status, luxury, and comfort to become "nobody" in a stable in Bethlehem. His Father did everything possible for him to live in total obscurity for thirty years. He then empowered him to demonstrate humility, love, compassion with authority, and sacrifice, culminating in a brutal death. Beaten by thugs and cheats, he appeared to have lost the game . . . until his resurrection three days later and the ultimate victory lap and celebration.

Friends and followers were captivated and inspired by what they witnessed in the life, death, and resurrection of Jesus. They had struggled themselves to hang in with him. They had failed to share his courage. They could not even comprehend what was going on. It took a while. Through the struggle, they began to know the love of God the Father gently inviting them into a new way of living.

It is clear to us that leaving nets and boats to follow him was a no-brainer. Their lives were never the same; those things that once held meaning paled into nothing compared to what Jesus evoked and released in them. Theirs were lives defined by passion, conviction, tenacity, sacrifice, and believing in something so much that nothing else mattered.

CONSIDER:

What about you? As you anticipate the rest of your life, how are you intending to invest your time, money, emotions, and passions? There is no right or wrong answer . . . or maybe there is. What we invest in something will determine what we get out of it. How much of *you* is invested in growing as a passionate, unselfish follower of Jesus? Is passion lopsided so that something, or someone, else evokes far more enthusiasm in our hearts than being Christian?

If that is the case, there is no point in beating ourselves up. Consider whether a clue to the shrinking enthusiasm may lie in a tendency to *fit God in* rather than taking time to invest. If Bateman seldom practiced with brush and pen, he would never be an accomplished artist. If Rory only held a golf club for an hour on Sundays and never loved the game, he wouldn't be at the top.

What one element of faith can you take hold of and practice this week which will demand a certain commitment and effort from you? Often, it is the small actions that have great consequences. It is time invested regularly that can help stimulate and grow our faith in Jesus.

2 Timothy 1:6

For this reason I remind you to fan into flame the gift of God, which is in you through the laying on of my hands.

34 | Easter

I LOVE EASTER—THE BIGGER-THAN-NUCLEAR blasting open of the tomb where the local bullies and the prince of darkness had stuffed the body of Jesus.

"Thank god he's dead!" they exclaimed, slapping high fives and zipping up their leather jackets, then speeding down to the local pub to celebrate, open throttles roaring. Good guys never win.

Meanwhile, the followers of Jesus were traumatized and broken. "It seemed so good for a while. We'd hoped . . . What's going to happen now?" They huddled in fear behind locked doors. In the long, dark silence between the bloody cross on Friday and the rolling stone on Sunday, God the Father was moving with power and passion—when everyone thought he was dead and doing nothing.

Then, like Aslan the lion in C.S. Lewis's novels, he roared. The heavens opened; light broke through the gloom and doom. Jesus appeared with scars from the battle and a triumphant smile.

"It is finished," he declared.

"What do you mean?" mumbled his disciples, uncertain of whether to laugh or cry, their nerves frayed, minds muddled, hearts thumping.

"The one who masquerades as the prince of this world is defeated; we've taken care of that. You need never be afraid again. All I have is yours, my peace is yours . . . Wait a while and you will receive my power to live extraordinary lives—in my name."

Easter is the day we celebrate God opening wide the gates of heaven and releasing his power into the world ("your Kingdom come, your will be done, on earth as in heaven"). Before Easter, humanity had survived on the embers of sacrifice, on rigid adherence to rules and rituals—all in the rather vague and forlorn hope of appeasing a distant deity. Church officials were his human face and self-appointed bodyguards; it was miserable. This was not God's will but satan's cunning strategy to encourage institutional religion and destroy every memory of the Creator as a personal and loving Father.

There's mystery in this big picture for sure, riddled with questions we will never answer, like so many things around us. Who knows the inner workings of cell phones, or how computer chips store so much information, or how hummingbirds can flap their wings so fast?

Easter is when God the Father declared, "Enough!" In that historic moment every human being has been invited to live life in relationship with him. In his company we experience power and decisive victory over the dark shadows of fear and insecurity threatening our very existence. The vanquished enemy will do anything possible to distract us from the truth and significance of the day of his defeat—even resorting to chocolates and colorful bunnies. He would rather we beat our chests at the foot of the cross for eternity, confessing our sin and feeling guilt. Religious prisoners in his grip will never enter life on earth with the risen and powerful Jesus, Lord of all! But . . .

The gates of heaven are wide open for all who will come. They are the naked cross and the empty grave—step through them and Jesus will welcome you home. He died physically so that we may come alive spiritually; that we may be confident in our identity as sons and daughters, in our purpose, and most importantly, what it means to be loved unconditionally and outrageously. Live life from a victory won on your behalf, rather than hoping to earn a victory dependent on your performance. We judge, discourage, or dismiss one another; God never does.

It is completed, available now. What on earth are we waiting for? I love Easter; every day, we get to rise! Enter in and receive your inheritance, possess the land, defeat the leather jackets—this is no place for chocolate bunnies! Every day of our lives after Easter is now hope-filled.

CONSIDER:

Are you living from a place of mercy, acceptance, grace, and where Jesus likes you and is a friend? Or do you still struggle to believe it is for you?

We cannot think our way into faith or even God's love. Faith is taken hold of, grabbed like a child, held close with affection. Believing is seeing.

1 JOHN 4:4

You, dear children, are from God and have overcome them, because the one who is in you is greater than the one who is in the world.

Love will find a way, indifference will find an excuse.

UKRAINIAN PROVERB

35 | Power

LIFE IN THE KINGDOM of God—on earth as in heaven—is quite different from us trying our best to please God or win his approval through religious ritual. It is effortlessly easy to be disheartened and frustrated, with a sense that you'll never make it, be good enough, feel spiritual, or "beat the battle within" to do your own thing. Our natural and normal default approach is to try harder and to distill Christianity down to performance or duty.

But take heart; there's good news. Instead of trying to read the Bible as a book of instructions impossible to follow, learn to love the learning. In other words, recognize that the Christian journey is a lifelong process that will always reveal our inability to accomplish what only God can do in us. Trying to be spiritual, or like Jesus, on our own is as futile as a lightbulb striving to shine by reflecting the sun. It cannot burn bright by merely reflecting its surroundings or circumstances.

The lightbulb must connect to a power source that releases light within to shine. It is dependent upon electricity to work and fulfil its purpose. So too are we dependent on a higher power. That truth and reality is not a source of shame, inadequacy, or personal failure; it is how we were created to be. To resignedly declare, "I'm not spiritual," is to miss the point. Be careful therefore not to give up or become discouraged. Keep coming back to ask yourself where your source of power is located.

Jesus came into the world to inspire and encourage, as well as to break down barriers that separate us from God the Father. He is like the great electrician after a power outage who rides into town and gets the plant up and running again. We often have power outages, when suddenly everything we depend upon and take for granted stops working. The fridge no longer hums, heating evaporates, and cold air muscles in at the first opportunity. Lights do not work, the computer shuts down, there is no power to make coffee, the water pump in the well does not send water flowing through the system . . .

When that happens, my response is not to kick the appliances, scream at them for not working, or berate them for causing me great inconvenience by their rebellious and uncooperative spirit. No, I do not scold an appliance for a power outage it has no control over. In the same way, we often get frustrated with ourselves and others causing untold grief and discouragement when we fail to check the power supply first! While we do not have control over a power outage, we do have control over whether we are plugged in or not.

When we feel powerless or overwhelmed, the wisdom is to check the plug first, rather than rationalize why nothing is working in me and through me. The learning is that only Jesus can produce life-changing fruit in me. Loving the learning means always starting with nurturing the relationship that Jesus invites us to enter into with him and his Father. They are more than willing to help us grow. They empower us to entertain possibilities we'd never have imagined if we insisted on remaining self-reliant.

In the Kingdom, God's power released in us is as radical and as real as access to unlimited electricity. Once the discovery is made, then the learning becomes an exciting adventure of how to harness this gift. The struggle in our understanding is that things are done differently: change is required, unlearning is normal, practice is routine, and then we can reasonably anticipate fruitfulness and better outcomes.

CONSIDER:

Instead of assuming there is more to be done to know God's power flowing in you and through you, believe that he has done enough and receive it as real and present for you now. Offer him thanks that he lives in you and empowers you. Of course, the process of yielding, refining, and releasing is lifelong. But he has given you more than enough for today.

LUKE 10:19

"I have given you authority to trample on snakes and scorpions and to overcome all the power of the enemy; nothing will harm you."

36 | Dinner at Simon's House

I AM THINKING ABOUT the evening when Jesus had supper with Simon, a very respected and obviously influential man about town. Simon's dinner parties were well known. To be invited was indeed an honor. He frequently opened his doors to visiting celebrities. Despite his protestations, that is what Jesus was fast becoming—what with all the healings and miracles. Simon lived for the applause and accolades of his peers. These dinner parties were more about his need to look important as a Pharisee of means and influence, than they were about appreciating the guest of honor.

When Jesus dined at Simon's table, he picked up on this but politely said nothing—until that woman of questionable background and notorious reputation (in Simon's eyes) became emotional. She was standing behind Jesus, at his feet (they reclined while eating). Suddenly she broke down and wept, anointing his feet with expensive perfume, and drying them with her hair. She could not stop saying "thank you," and Jesus did not interrupt her. He knew what was transpiring in her heart, and this outpouring of emotion was entirely appropriate. She had been lost and was now found; she had been condemned and was now forgiven, fully accepted into the heart of the Father. Jesus knew what she knew, but Simon did not have a clue. All he could think about was how wicked she was and the awkward scene she was creating in his carefully orchestrated evening. It certainly wasn't great for his image.

Jesus read Simon's mind and registered his horrified expression—which is why he addressed it publicly. Jesus said that what the woman had done was far more authentic and hospitable than Simon's superficial fawning and egocentric hospitality. The woman was set free that evening. Simon, unfortunately, remained imprisoned because he could not see beyond himself. Perhaps later he reflected on the events and had a change of heart—we do not know. But that day, a woman who had devalued her worth and lost her identity was loved by a man who did not use her or abuse her. Jesus touched the innermost depth of her heart that screamed, "Is there any hope for me, is there anyone out there who cares?" His response was not a syrupy spiritual "God loves you, smile, be happy" sort of sentimental drivel. It was powerful and strong. His words stood up in the face of those who would shame her; and with massive power behind his deceptive gentleness, Jesus restored to her life, dignity, and respect.

I celebrate the fact that Jesus is not at all religious. He genuinely enjoys hanging out with people who are real and authentic. He is not politically correct, and he loves to lift people up who have gotten down or lost for all kinds of reasons. He seems quite prepared to get in the face of self-important people and challenge them. It is so refreshing, don't you think, so fearless.

Jesus ended his conversation with Simon by saying that those who have been forgiven much love passionately. They weep and sing, they dance and shout, they laugh and cry. They express their relief and joy and delight. That does not mean we all have to be the same. But for God's sake, if we have been recued from death, surely something can be squeezed out of us that demonstrates gratitude and excitement?

Simon liked to talk about theology, and what Jesus was up to, and how people were responding. He gave Jesus his dinner table, his conversation, and his mind. But he withheld his heart. The woman had no table or home, but she gave Jesus all she had: a heart filled with gratitude and the perfume—the tools of her trade—to be redeemed. Jesus was moved, thrilled, delighted, and commended her in front of all who condemned her.

CONSIDER:

How strong is your passion, and how much of you does Jesus have? I want him to have all of me. I am still learning how to walk into that truth. I know how he has loved me when others were far away. He has never abandoned me. I love him for that gift, with unspeakable gratitude.

LUKE 7:44–47

Then [Jesus] turned toward the woman and said to Simon, "Do you see this woman? I came into your house. You did not give me any water for my feet, but she wet my feet with her tears and wiped them with her hair. You did not give me a kiss, but this woman, from the time I entered, has not stopped kissing my feet. You did not put oil on my head, but she has poured perfume on my feet. Therefore, I tell you, her many sins have been forgiven—as her great love has shown. But whoever has been forgiven little loves little."

---

*If you can walk you can dance.
If you can talk you can sing.*

ZIMBABWE PROVERB

---

37 | Ask and Receive

Sometimes God calms the storm around us. Sometimes he allows that storm to rage as he calms the storm within us.

The secret to weathering the chaos of storms in our circumstances and personal lives is found in our relationship with Jesus, rather than in our ability to design and build elaborate shelters and escape routes. You will probably have noticed that this emphasis on a relationship with Jesus is a frequent theme in these writings. That is because the relationship is the bedrock of everything. His faithfulness, trustworthiness, and strength are enough for everything we will encounter.

When I nearly drowned in a rip-out current off the South African coast, I felt the panic rise. I cried out to God, "Is this it, how I'm to end my life?" The answer came in a whisper within. "Keep calm, conserve your breath, stay afloat, rescue is on its way." I treaded water for about five minutes before a surfer sliced through the waves, and within a few minutes we were back on solid ground. The experience has remained with me as an example of trusting in another when my strength and capacity to overcome my circumstances are not enough.

That is what Jesus meant when he said, "I can do nothing by myself." Life on the rock is about being assured of my identity as God our Father's beloved son; being confident that he always has his eye on me, his ear bent toward me. He will not always change my circumstances, but he will always provide me with what I need to make it through—one way or another. I do not know how many times in my life it's felt so slow in coming!

Jesus told us that each of us has a room awaiting us in heaven. Our room in heaven is filled with resources that are unavailable on earth. In our room there is peace bearing the hallmark of Jesus—which means it is a collector's item on earth—personally customized, impossible to replicate.

It is accessed by faith and released to me when I ask the Father. It is priceless, powerful, exceptionally durable, and stronger than any circumstance I'll ever encounter on earth where fear or anxiety is present.

Isn't that presumptuous? Not at all, if what we ask is healthy, and good for us and others. Jesus said, "Ask and it will be given to you; seek and you will find; knock and the door will be opened to you . . . If you, then, though you are evil, know how to give good gifts to your children, how much more will your Father in heaven give good gifts to those who ask him!" (Matthew 7:7, 11).

The same is true for love, joy, patience, kindness, long-suffering, perseverance, forgiveness, and power. Our heavenly rooms are filled to overflowing with resources ready to be utilized anytime we choose . . . on earth as in heaven. Everything I encounter on earth has a provision for me to access through Jesus—made in heaven. It is delivered invisibly at my request. The more I receive and believe, the stronger it grows within me.

The implication is that we are to live during uncertainty and even hostility confident in the rock of God's faithfulness, his love, his care, his provision, and his presence. We hold tightly to him and lightly to things, as we learn to walk in peace and the assurance of his provision along the way. Rejoice!

CONSIDER:

If you are struggling with thoughts about your future, ask for faith and hope. Then, give thanks for the gift of faith, believing that Jesus has your future in his hands and that your hope for positive outcomes is secure with him. Believe that he says, "yes." Ask him to help you see his answers for you day by day, in the ordinary. It may be a conversation or something you see on TV. It could be a friendship or a chance meeting with someone. You may need encouragement from those around you as you walk and grow, which is one of the reasons God draws us into community as we travel with him.

Matthew 7:8–9

For everyone who asks receives; the one who seeks finds; and to the one who knocks, the door will be opened. "Which of you, if your son asks for bread, will give him a stone?"

38 | Facing Fear

What difference does the resurrection of Jesus make?

One of the most significant ways I have been impacted by the resurrection is how I have experienced fear diminish in many areas of my life. I am not talking about a healthy fear of danger such as caution with fire, or wild animals. That is normal and serves us well.

As a child I was asthmatic, extremely nervous, and fearful. In my early twenties when considering full-time ministry, I was terrified of public speaking, afraid I would not measure up, and in some confusion about my identity and self-worth.

Fear is a debilitating presence that manifests in our lives as insecurity, shyness, reluctance to try new things, and avoidance of commitment. It is probably attached to a wide variety of other habits and behaviors. One of the hallmarks of someone struggling with fear is often discovered lurking beneath anger. Other clues to symptoms of fear could be:

- anxiety,
- worrying about what others think,
- lack of trust,
- reluctance to volunteer,
- inability to take responsibility for one's actions,
- selfishness,
- a critical spirit (always blaming or finding fault),
- and the list goes on.

We would probably all agree that these are rather negative behavior patterns, aren't they? Not the way I would want to be remembered at all. Yet it is not so easy to escape fear's tentacles.

Perhaps the antidote to fear is like getting rid of fleas on a cat. Imagine how laborious it would be to take hold of your favorite pet and try to eradicate fleas by chasing after each one; your life would be consumed with the effort. A better way is to have the vet inject an anti-flea medication that enters the bloodstream and kills the fleas as they bite. When Jesus poured out his Spirit on all people and invited us into a personal relationship, the promise was released declaring that his perfect love casts out all fear.

An effective way to combat fear is not to focus too long on what is causing fear. Affirm your relationship with Jesus and allow his love to fill you to overflowing. His love comes with power, security, assurance, and protection; with the understanding that you are not alone.

Fear will weaken its grip. Then all it takes are a few steps courageously forward and it will flee. Those few steps are important. We often think that the experience of freedom comes without action; it seldom does. Intentional faith is how we clinch the deal and find victory. Faith is doing something in response to Jesus, even if we feel afraid. We are declaring that his faithfulness will ultimately triumph.

What does that look like?

CONSIDER:

Ask God what fear he is releasing you from. Or ask yourself in what areas of your life fear is getting in the way of moving forward. Where is fear inhibiting or discouraging you? What can you do to defeat it? Perhaps it is admitting it to yourself, asking for help from a friend, or sharing with another how you feel. Be authentic and bring it to light. Refuse to allow pride or perfection to keep fear in the dark where it thrives.

The answer will be easy to hear. It is whichever one you are most aware of. If, like I was, you are afraid of speaking in front of others, then begin to step out and speak whenever you have the opportunity. It is normal to be nervous, but you will never experience God's faithfulness and peace without taking some risk. When fear threatens you with disaster and defeat, love will bless you with boldness and increasing confidence. The same will be true with finances, plans, and ministry of any description.

Take the pressure off yourself by admitting to others that you are nervous or fearful. Do not seek perfection; it is normal to make mistakes as we learn. Sharing our weaknesses is what authenticity is about, and others will meet us more than halfway. Perhaps it would be better for us to declare that we are "practicing Christians."

Philippians 4:6–7

Do not be anxious about anything, but in every situation, by prayer and petition, with thanksgiving, present your requests to God. And the peace of God, which transcends all understanding, will guard your hearts and your minds in Christ Jesus.

39 | Overcoming Timidity

Passivity is waiting for God, or others, to do something so that our lives will be better. Timidity is when we hold back because we are afraid, do not feel worthy, or are unsure of the response we will receive. Perhaps it is evidence of lack of trust in God's faithfulness. It could be for many reasons, such as believing lies about ourselves and even God. Timidity is a common challenge for all who want to know God and follow him.

Moses was afraid. He was a goatherder for forty years before he was called to shepherd the captive Hebrews from slavery in Egypt to freedom. Joshua was encouraged on numerous occasions to be courageous. He had to fill the shoes of Moses and lead the liberated Hebrews into the Promised Land. Gideon was riddled with a sense of inferiority when commissioned to lead men into battle. Isaiah felt very unworthy when he was anointed as a prophet. David experienced bouts of despair as he was fulfilling his destiny to be the king of Israel. Mary and Joseph were terrified and way out of their depth when they contemplated the birth of Jesus as their son. The shepherds trembled when an angel appeared in their field inviting them to witness the birth of God's Son in Bethlehem. Years later, the disciples roller-coastered through unbelief, confusion, amazement, and huge disillusionment. Saul/Paul tumbled from arrogant certainty into an abyss of blindness and new revelation as he encountered a God so much larger than his small Jewish paradigm and tiny intellect.

The conclusion I draw is that if we never feel out of our depth, afraid or timid in our relationship with God, we are probably not following him. The good news is that timidity can be an encouraging sign to help us move toward growth, or the willingness to be stretched, if we are alive to God.

A few years ago, a group of us from the church decided to offer prayers for healing at a local summer street market every Tuesday evening. I asked God for words of knowledge—a picture of someone who perhaps needed encouragement and did not know God cares. I did not want to go through the whole summer standing beside a banner broadcasting healing and not grow myself. Before the Tuesday evening, I sat quietly for fifteen minutes and asked Jesus for pictures. On the last two evenings, I had pictures of various people and a word for them. It would always feel as if I were just making it up, but I now know sometimes it's my imagination and sometimes it is God. Both start off feeling much the same. The only way to grow is to go with what you have, no matter what. God loves to communicate with us and do good works through us; it is our unbelief and overthinking that often gets in the way.

The first week one of the pictures was of a woman wearing fuchsia-colored shoes. Halfway through the evening a woman in green pants and fuchsia shoes walked by, being pulled by a little dog. I saw her but did not have the nerve to stop her and talk. The following Tuesday I had another picture of fuchsia shoes. I had just parked the car when a businesswoman walked past me dressed in a black power suit. She was clicking down the road wearing the loudest fuchsia shoes you could imagine. Again, I backed off, wondering how I could stop her and ask a crazy question about trauma in her life. I allowed timidity to steal the possibility of an encounter with God. Does that mean I am feeling guilty and depressed today? Not at all!

Yes, I was kicking myself for a while that I chickened out. But . . . I am on a journey to grow in this area. I wouldn't even have experienced timidity if I'd not said to the Lord, "I want words of knowledge for people I don't know." At least I had a few pictures and I saw someone who may have fitted the description. That is a start. I am inching into boldness. The learning curve to grow faith and boldness is the same for almost everything we attempt as we practice following and obeying the leading of Jesus. It is a battle between our inadequacy and our trust in his promises and faithfulness to be present and active precisely at our point of weakness. Leaps of faith invariably begin with something that sounds crazy.

CONSIDER:

Why not think of a person you care about who may need encouragement? Ask God for a picture, or a word, and see what happens. Write down what comes to mind and reflect about whether there is something there that will bless the person. Ask God for a picture for yourself as well. You do not have to embellish; merely share the impression by saying to the person that you are practicing hearing God, and this is what you think he might be saying. See how they respond and learn from there.

MATTHEW 14:31

Immediately Jesus reached out his hand and caught him. "You of little faith," he said, "why did you doubt?"

---

*Hunger is felt by a slave
and hunger is felt by a king.*

GHANAIAN PROVERB

40 | Dare to Try

Have you ever confided something personal to someone that was important to you, only for them to break your confidence and share what you told them in front of others? How did that make you feel? What does it mean to be truthful, vulnerable, and trusting? Fear is often rooted in the lie that we are different from everyone else, and no one struggles or messes up like we do. Everyone has strengths and weaknesses. What if it does not matter what others think so long as we are authentic and honest ourselves?

I have mentioned before that I used to be terrified of speaking publicly. I wrote long notes, wished the time to speak was over, laboriously researched to be relevant, and so on. It was the practice of doing that released the confidence to be and become. The same has been true for leading worship, praying in public, laying hands on the sick, and even resting in silence and believing when nothing seems to be happening.

In my personal life, I have been terrified of not having enough, worrying about how my future would unfold. Experiencing God's provision and faithfulness demands that I step out of the boat (for me, fear of not having enough; yours may look different). Timidity is what Paul wrote about to his young friend Timothy. He exhorted him to not be timid or ashamed of the gospel. "For the Spirit God gave us does not make us timid, but gives us power, love and self-discipline" (2 Timothy 1:7). In the previous verse, Paul reminds Timothy (St. Timidity) to fan into flames the gift of God which was in him through the laying on of hands.

The implication is that, even with gifts imparted to us by God's Spirit, there is a process to growth and maturity. Gifts are seldom if ever delivered in mature form. They are not always obvious and require encouragement and a safe place to nurture and blossom. That might mean watching someone more advanced in that field. It means being mentored, learning by doing, and making mistakes. It means growing in confidence, as the way God teaches one person may not be the same for another. Love is always the foundation, respect for others paramount, and encouragement and blessing the goal. Dialing down our insecurity and apprehension about God using us the same as he did the first disciples is our greatest hurdle.

Authenticity is a powerful antidote to timidity, especially within a church context where community is foundational.

It means learning to say what we think to one another, to actively listen, and to pursue multiple conversations. If we are united in wanting to discern God's heart, we won't mind being right or wrong. We will grow to know and believe that what we have to say is a worthy contribution toward a greater whole. It may be risky—but not for long. We want to grow a culture in which we can risk and fail responsibly, and experience extravagant grace. We want to nurture an encouraging atmosphere where we can disagree without the fear of rejection or requiring months of therapy because we did not get what we wanted.

CONSIDER:

Let us encourage one another to face our fears, rather than retreat and be imprisoned by what we perceive to be our limitations. Beware of assuming you know how others will respond. Choose not to blame the lack in others to justify your own timidity. Set the bar higher for what is possible in you and through you. That is why we need others to call out of us what we struggle to believe—yet. And our interconnectedness may well mean that our key to breakthrough is also linked to the obedience of someone else, and vice versa.

Are we teachable, humble, hungry for more, available, and a little daring? Can we show up and contend for others, often? Can we give generously, serve willingly, receive with gratitude, and expect "so much more than we can imagine for one another"? I sure hope so.

Isaiah 40:31

. . . those who hope in the Lord will renew their strength. They will soar on wings like eagles; they will run and not grow weary; they will walk and not be faint.

41 | WHY CHURCH?

I HAVE OFTEN WONDERED how Jesus tolerated and endured his twenty-five years in Nazareth, particularly as he grew older and worked as a carpenter in the village. It is widely thought that Joseph died some time before Jesus began his public ministry at the age of thirty—which would have placed responsibility for the family upon Jesus' shoulders.

Imagine having an increasing sense of your destiny and a spiritual insight totally off the radar screen of your peers. Probably most of the people Jesus grew up with would have been married with children by the time he was in his late twenties. He understood a thing or two about being single, no sex before marriage, coping with unfulfilled longings, and being patient. Instead of being "holier than thou" and contemptuous of the "small-box thinking" of his contemporaries, Jesus' friendship with them no doubt kept him from becoming unbearable to live with. He understood the nature of the battle and certainly realized with increasing revelation that his purpose was ultimately to set captives free and provide a solution.

If anyone had the right to say that he and God had a special relationship—it was Jesus. "I don't need to be part of anything. Religious people are inconsistent and hypocritical . . . " Those words could have spilled from his lips. Instead, we read in Luke's account of Jesus that it was his custom to attend synagogue every Sabbath. In doing so he was affirming a core value of God's heart for his people—to appreciate how much we need one another and to not neglect meeting together.

Sadly, many of us have negative experiences regarding church, and all too frequently opting out seems a valid response. But just as an abusive father is an aberration of what a good, loving father should be, challenging encounters with church do not invalidate God's intent. I believe he wants us to experience a healthy family gathering where interdependency, humility, servanthood, friendship, and mutual encouragement are what bind us together. Church should be a place where we encourage each other, learn together, and challenge each other to apply our faith to the wider world with confidence and excitement.

Reasons for gathering might include:

Mutual encouragement—supporting one another as we explore faith, encounter challenges, and ask questions, sometimes difficult ones, with the understanding that everyone has their ups and downs as followers of Jesus.

Worship—declaring truths of God the Father's love and character through music, prayer, and participation with others. Much like watching a sporting event in a crowded stadium is more exciting than watching it on TV alone, so too can group worship be more enriching and meaningful than praying solo.

Learning—studying and discussing what the Bible says and how it applies in our context today. Learning together can help us to build a foundation on God's word and promises rather than our feelings.

Prayer and healing—experiencing the presence and power of God firsthand; he continues to heal today!

Serving—offering to serve others. In this way we can truly live out our purpose as God's servants, spreading his message through our actions, not just our words.

Friendship—building relationships, learning to hear God, and believing that he will work in and through any of us who are willing and open.

Financial support—pooling our resources so that we can finance and support much more than is possible individually.

Breaking bread together at the Lord's Supper—following another core value that Jesus instructed his disciples to take seriously as a tangible expression of his presence among them, to the end of the age.

And most challenging of all—church is a community where we *witness one another's imperfections*, get irritated and impatient, and can extend grace and forgiveness.

CONSIDER:

Talk to Jesus about how you are experiencing "church." Are you loving your connection, are you bruised and withdrawn, or perhaps indifferent or lukewarm? Wherever you are, he will understand and empathetically listen. There is no condemnation or pressure. Be still and hear what he has to say to you, his dearly beloved son or daughter.

HEBREWS 10:24–25

And let us consider how we may spur one another on toward love and good deeds, not giving up meeting together, as some are in the habit of doing, but encouraging one another—and all the more as you see the Day approaching.

42 | NEVER INSIGNIFICANT

MY INSPIRATION FOR THIS reflection comes from the singer/songwriter Matt Redman, as he describes the meaning of "Mirror Ball," the title of one of his books.

He talks about working with Louis Giglio (pastor of the large Passion Church in Atlanta) to host a massive worship celebration for students, giving God as much glory as Taylor Swift had received in the same venue a few days earlier. "People love to party, so why can't we be loud and expressive when we gather before God—at least sometimes?" Redman asked. As part of that great celebration, Louis was enthused about using a mirror ball to add to the sense of wonder and occasion. At the rehearsal beforehand Matt saw the tiny object waiting to be lowered into place and thought there was no way it was going to create the impact Louis expected. "I wanted to laugh but didn't want to hurt Louis' feelings," he said.

Celebration time arrived, and sure enough, halfway through the program strong beams of light were aimed at the mirror ball. "The entire arena exploded into a mass of moving lights striking everyone's faces and lighting up the atmosphere. It was amazing to see," Matt recounted. "I was wrong because my focus had been on the insignificant size of the mirror ball. I forgot to factor in the power and impact of the light." He explained how God can use anyone who is willing to be aligned with him; how, when his light shines on us, and through us, the impact will be beyond our comprehension or understanding.

It has always been that way.

Paul talks about God using humble uneducated men and women to reflect his light and form the foundation of the early church. God encourages us to believe in what he can do in us and through us—today, now.

He's calling "time out" on our excuses and inviting us to step in, step out, and trust him with the consequences. It is an exciting invitation.

There is nothing more wasted than a mirror ball hanging around with no light shining on it. Take away the light and it is nothing much at all. Matt insists that passion is the key to radiantly reflecting God's light in the world. The greatest example is Jesus, who so loved us that he laid down his life, endured the cross, and was resurrected that we may know hope and have a glorious present/future.

Louis Giglio defines passion as whatever it takes to accomplish something despite significant obstacles, challenges, or hurdles. So often we use passion to describe what we like doing—what we "feel passionate about"—but this definition takes us much deeper. It reveals to us the heart of God and the cost of following Jesus. Passion for something worthwhile inevitably includes effort, sacrifice, endurance, and even inconvenience.

"But it's worth it!" we exclaim with joy.

CONSIDER:

Are you perhaps feeling unseen, or unappreciated, like a mirror ball with no light? Or are you in a season where you are just enduring? Don't give up—Jesus sees us when we lose sight of him. Everything takes time. What is a strong interest, talent, or passion you have? It could be a desire to teach, help others, learn to play an instrument, build something... Try to find someone who is more advanced or somewhere you can grow, practice, learn, or serve. Watch what happens and enjoy the process.

ROMANS 15:13

May the God of hope fill you with all joy and peace as you trust in him, so that you may overflow with hope by the power of the Holy Spirit.

43 | The Impact of Jesus

"I wasn't expecting this!" is a phrase that often escapes our lips when we agree to start something only to find a few surprises around the first corner. That is what makes life such an adventure. A relationship with Jesus can be unpredictable. We are in good company. The Bible shows us that the early disciples were constantly stretched, overwhelmed, nervous, and astounded in their walk alongside Jesus. By contrast, things that do not move, are never surprising, are not open to change, we call . . . dead.

How we think and what we believe influences what we do. If what we believe does not reflect truth, then what we feel will not reflect our distorted reality. Truth that ignores God becomes whatever we can figure out, or explain within the limits of our minds, perceptions, and worldviews. Truth with God as an external source to us is something we are constantly discovering and growing into. We recognize our limitations and therefore happily acknowledge that our thoughts and feelings are not always reliable or trustworthy.

Wherever Jesus went there was life in all its complexity—intrigue, confrontation, revelation, healing, anger, forgiveness, paradigm shifts, and people amazed. His life was the most perfect expression of the fullness of God in human form ever witnessed. While it is a model and yardstick, we know that even as we aspire to be like him, such perfection is beyond our grasp. However, it is a direction we are invited to move toward. Knowing that, one might conclude that communities of believers today would evoke a similar excitement and be powerhouses of passion—because Jesus is alive and roaring like a lion in them and through them. Sadly, that is seldom the case. Too often we find people huddled in clusters just trying to survive, intimidated by a gigantic world and a dwarf-sized Jesus.

It is somewhat reminiscent of the first Hebrew settlers in the Promised Land. They were not expecting challenges. They exaggerated the power of those they were meant to conquer. Over four thousand years later, the world is still a broken and disfigured wasteland desperately needing salt and light. People are scared spitless of sickness and cancer—Jesus heals. Vast numbers live in bondage to drugs, alcohol, sex, and countless addictions—Jesus sets captives free. And when there is no healing on earth, or freedom from addiction, Jesus does not turn away. He has conquered death, and his resurrection demonstrates that there is a life beyond. Because of him, death is not the end.

Today, followers of Jesus are meant to be the "in person" revelation of God's love that Jesus embodied when he walked the earth—to strangers, and to one another.

Men and woman live without hope in broken relationships, abused, lonely, trying to make it through another day—Jesus comforts. Many have poor self-esteem and little sense of worth or identity—Jesus introduces us to the Father of the fatherless. Others live with shame and guilt locked up within—Jesus forgives. Some live hedonistic lifestyles where their sole priority is fun and self-gratification—Jesus opens the eyes of the blind. Respectable people ensure they have what they need, working hard and storing much (addicted to greed and selfishness)—Jesus dismantles strongholds. The fields are still ripe for the harvest and the workers are few.

How did Jesus make such an impact and accomplish so much in such a short life? He loved the world so passionately that he became as one of us, living among us, declaring the Kingdom of God to be near, demonstrating its presence and power. He called the same broken people who were transformed by his presence and power to follow him and pass on what they had received: to reach out to the lost, heal the sick, cast out demons, and bear witness to the Kingdom come.

This mandate was called the gospel (good news), with the first two letters of that word propelling us into action—"Go!" Imagine if all the disciples did was to approach wounded people with a smile and a sandwich and declare the Kingdom of God was present in their midst. They would not have needed Jesus' life, death, and resurrection for that, or the Holy Spirit.

Where the "Go" of the gospel kicked in was when power was released to impact hearts and lives.

CONSIDER:

The Holy Spirit comes with power for healing, love, revelation, and personal experience, resulting in lasting transformation. The Spirit usually comes to us through other people and then flows out to others even when we are unaware—when Jesus lives within us.

The tap looked up at the tank filled with water and said, "I wish I had all the water you have."

"You can have it all," replied the tank. "Just open up and it will flow through you."

JOHN 14:12–14

Very truly I tell you, whoever believes in me will do the works I have been doing, and they will do even greater things than these, because I am going to the Father. And I will do whatever you ask in my name, so that the Father may be glorified in the Son. You may ask me for anything in my name, and I will do it.

44 | God's Green Fingers

Some people are amazing with gardens.

They see potential in an overgrown mass of foliage and a tangle of bush weeds. Give them a few tools and witness the transformation. It will not be long before pools flow amid what were barren rocks, roses bloom, and fruit trees spread their branches over lawns fringed with every color in the rainbow. Same ground below and sky above, transformed by the vision and labor of the one who cares for it.

Jesus spoke about his Father being a gardener. He identified himself as a vine in his Father's garden. He was reliant upon his Father to sustain him and to nurture the life that flowed through him. He described those who followed him as branches attached to the vine (Jesus) in the same garden—that could be you and me. They are equally cared for and nurtured, so that from the vine of Jesus and through the branches (us) fruit can form and grow to maturity. It is another metaphor for life and purpose.

Every seed planted contains a particular flower or fruit that bursts into bloom and beauty after planting, watering, and patient gardening. Included in the process is weeding, pruning, and fertilizing in order that everything stored within that tiny seed will be released. I often think about this when I become discouraged or overwhelmed. On one such occasion, God showed me a wildly overgrown garden where all that was visible were knotted vines and weeds. That so often resembles the clutter and chaos of someone's life.

"Look for the shoots of the flowers and fruit trees underneath," he said. "Nurture the life that perhaps is not clearly visible yet. Give others a vision for a landscape and garden they cannot see or believe for themselves. Keep describing what you see and watch the new life begin to break through the jungle."

Such a revelation has not come easily or quickly for me. Too often the weeds and the struggles have preoccupied me and borne the brunt of my complaining. I have hacked at the thorn bushes, thinking that once they are cleared I will be able to plant a garden. The problem usually is that because the cutting and clearing have taken so much energy, I have lost sight of the ultimate vision.

God reminded me that he approaches gardening quite differently. The rain falls on the weeds and the wheat (or flowers) until the harvest (Matthew 13:29). He allows both to grow together, primarily because in the early stages the weeds and "good plants" can look very similar. As they mature, their true nature and identity is revealed. It is an encouraging reminder to me about where to focus and whom to trust with the landscaping and development of my life—as well as the lives of those around me.

Patience and consistency are required, while resisting the urge to jump to conclusions or make hasty judgments. We must learn to focus on the bigger picture—the ultimate vision—trusting the head gardener with the management of the process. We must allow for seasons of pruning, rest, fruitfulness, and new beginnings. Different plants and fruits blossom and ripen at different times, all contributing as they do so. There is a great deal going on in any garden. The cycle of life and death, blooming and pruning, never ends. Often the most beautiful gardens are not well manicured or perfect. They reflect the personality and creativity of the gardener; some like it tidy and others, not so much. There's room for both, and all.

CONSIDER:

Wherever you happen to be today, stand in the rain of God's provision. Trust him, be patiently soaked in his love, and believe for what is not yet visible in you and those among whom you are planted. And if you're in a season of pruning, rejoice at what is to come. There's a purpose; it is not the end, and neither is it punishment.

JOHN 15:1–5

"I am the true vine, and my Father is the gardener. He cuts off every branch in me that bears no fruit, while every branch that does bear fruit he prunes so that it will be even more fruitful. You are already clean because of the word I have spoken to you. Remain in me, as I also remain in you. No

branch can bear fruit by itself; it must remain in the vine. Neither can you bear fruit unless you remain in me. I am the vine; you are the branches. If you remain in me and I in you, will bear much fruit; apart from me you can do nothing."

---

*A bird does not sing because it has an answer.
It sings because it has a song.*

CHINESE PROVERB

---

45 | Faith and Money

So how do we know when we are walking by faith, running ahead and being stupid, or dragging our feet because we are too scared to take a risk?

When pondering an exciting initiative, it does not take long before the topic of money is raised. "How much will it cost? Can we afford it right now? Is that the best use of our resources? What about . . . ?" It is as predictable as clockwork.

Money, when untamed, runs wild, a brute of a beast—rude, interruptive, and desiring to be the center of attention with the controlling vote. Jesus placed money in its rightful position as a servant, not a master. He delighted in living in a manner that dethroned what he named "the spirit of mammon." He had a fish deliver a coin into Peter's hand to satisfy the tax man, and he provided lunch for nearly ten thousand people without spending a cent. When Mary poured expensive perfume over Jesus' feet, some of the disciples were aghast at the waste. He responded by praising Mary for her extravagant offering, thereby indicating from God's perspective an entirely different set of priorities and values. Makes it confusing at times, doesn't it?

"Trust God," some respond. "Look to him first and the money will follow." "Yes, but you have to be sensible, God doesn't ask us to place our minds on the shelf," another replies. "Hey, God is giving us favor," someone else shouts with a smile. "Live on the edge, take some risks, look what he's already provided!" On an individual level and as a community, this can be a vexing challenge.

Whom does a person listen to? One of the truths we are learning is to be stern when money interjects too loudly and drowns everyone else out. In our Western culture it has been the bully, the king, and the CEO for far too long. It abuses some and elevates others. When Jesus takes ground for the Kingdom, money is one of the first dictators to be dethroned and put in its rightful place. "My Father knows what you need," Jesus reminds us. "Draw close to him, seek first his Kingdom, and watch how everything flows from that."

Once money is quietened, other voices are heard more easily. It is in the wider conversation that discernment, wisdom, and life-changing faith are nurtured and released. Here are a few suggestions regarding discernment that could apply to an individual within a circle of friends or a community. Discernment about the tug of money, unhealthy agendas, self-interest, bad habits—the hard things that inhibit transparency, community, and spiritual growth.

Whatever we think God may be saying to us about such matters, or our community, it is important to test that belief with others we know and trust. Refrain from saying, "God told me." Rather, be humble by saying, "I think this is what God may be saying."

It is always good to consider pragmatic reasoning and keep our perspective aligned with the big picture or vision arising from core values. They are there to keep us on track without necessitating that we start from scratch with every decision and challenge. The voice from Scripture and history ensures we are in alignment with historic Christian values. Teaching on Christian principles is important.

The safest place for discernment and God's timing to be captured and embraced is within the context of community or among trusted friends. Where relationships are healthy, the exchange of ideas, dreams, passions, and ministry development will be stimulating and fun. It is not unusual for the idea to be good and timing to be "the thing."

CONSIDER:

Is there anything in your life or church that is on hold because of finances? Perhaps there is an invitation to test God and ask again?

MALACHI 3:10

"Bring the whole tithe into the storehouse, that there may be food in my house. Test me in this," says the Lord Almighty, "and see if I will not throw open the floodgates of heaven and pour out so much blessing that there will not be room enough to store it."

46 | Ready, or Not?

Almost everything in the natural world we inhabit contains metaphors and insights that God can use to teach us about the invisible—where his Kingdom towers above and beyond anything we could comprehend or dream of.

Jesus talked about the lilies of the field being clothed in splendor and turned it into a promise of God's care and provision for us. He observed a sunset (they glow bright and orange over Galilee) and spoke about our ability to read weather patterns but not comprehend the "signs of the times." He watched a widow place two pennies in the offering plate and used it as an illustration of generosity and an example of how the Father sees every detail and motive arising from our hearts. At a dinner party he watched guests vying for the best seats and used it as an opportunity to caution his listeners against only looking after their own interests.

Recently, I sat in the atrium of the hospital awaiting multiple tests as part of an annual medical check-up for old men. I was told, "Take a number and wait . . . " for medical imaging; "Take a number and wait . . . " for cardiac tests and blood samples. "These are the tests we are doing," the doctor informed me, "to ensure there's no cancer present and your diet is healthy given your blood pressure is a little high." Off I went clutching blue forms, white forms, pink forms. A great deal of effort, concern, finances, and expertise are expended to keep this aging body walking and breathing.

As I sat clutching my number, I pondered what it would be like to have diagnostics for spiritual health—regular tests to see how strong my spirit is beating, to what extent attitudes and sin are clogging the arteries, to gauge the impact of my exercise in worship and praise. We could test for servant hearts, hope and passion, the level of forgiveness, and the amount of faith present. Then we get to sit down with an expert and discuss the results and how we can continue to grow and prepare for life beyond this mortal flesh.

Airports trigger a similar response in me. Imagine sitting in the departure lounge holding your number and waiting to pass through death.

"I've had a really healthy body most of my life and I'm extremely well educated," I say.

"Thanks very much for that information, sir, but right now it's not relevant to where you're going. We're screening your Spirit," the official informs me with an earnest expression. "Peter, can you come over here a minute? I'm struggling to pick up much here."

Someone rushes over and peers into the screen. He looks at me, puzzled. "What did you do to your Spirit? It's hardly visible the most important part of you from here on."

I begin to panic as suddenly everything comes into focus. My life flashes before my eyes, just like people say it does. I hear the man's voice who sat next to me in the hospital awaiting heart monitoring, saying, "I'm an atheist, science is discovering more every day about the universe... don't believe in God."

"What are you looking for?" I whisper, panic deflating my ability to shout.

"Wait a minute," says Peter. "I've enlarged the image; here's the cross, not much bigger than a mustard seed, but it's enough." He smiles. "We're searching for evidence of faith, anything that indicates the presence of Jesus in you. By the look of it, you're needing a miracle of grace to make this trip." I sigh with relief.

The doctor says, "Please don't leave what's most important to the very last minute."

CONSIDER:

If you were having a spiritual check-up today, what would you anticipate hearing from the specialist? Would you be fearful, or eager to know what you can do? The Holy Spirit will quietly show you, with no judgment or condemnation, merely a diagnosis and an invitation.

MATTHEW 25:1–5

At that time the kingdom of heaven will be like ten virgins who took their lamps and went out to meet the bridegroom. Five of them were foolish and five were wise. The foolish ones took their lamps but did not take any oil with them. The wise ones, however, took oil in jars along with their lamps. The bridegroom was a long time in coming, and they all became drowsy and fell asleep.

A half-truth is a whole lie.
JEWISH PROVERB

---

47 | COMMUNITY

COMMUNITY IS POWERFUL. It is the context in which God has chosen to mature and grow disciples—around his Son, Jesus. Whenever someone expresses an interest in Jesus, his Spirit tugs them by invisible threads toward a fellowship of believers. It is one of the ways we sense the Spirit of God. He loves company, relationships, and having people walk alongside each other—and him. That is why Jesus was surrounded by disciples for his entire ministry on earth. He wanted, and needed, company. And as they shared life, teaching moments occurred with great frequency. Why is that?

It is because Jesus desired those who followed him to be different from the many religious teachers he encountered in his travels—those who spent their lives fixated on the Scriptures, arguing about interpretation and ritual rather than allowing the Spirit of God to transform their hearts. Jesus taught his disciples while they were on the road, as they responded to circumstances, attitudes, opposition, hardship, victory, and one another. There is a massive difference between the classroom and the marketplace. Religious teachers and leaders tend to focus on information-gathering. Jesus embraced teaching but modeled application in the marketplace.

It is no surprise therefore when we find the same principle and dynamic happening in our lives. One of the ways we can talk to God about what he is transforming in our hearts is to pay attention to relationships. What is causing tension and why? What is frustrating me in this circumstance, and what is God trying to communicate to me about his love and purpose? Remember the men who lowered their friend, the paralyzed man, through the roof? They were desperate enough to believe that Jesus could heal and brought their sick friend to him. This act contrasted with spiritual leaders gathered around Jesus, questioning, and talking—almost certainly too afraid, or proud, to test and apply their belief that God can heal today before their eyes.

The key to freedom is being eager to learn and non-defensive when engaged in the process. Ask lots of questions. That is how Peter became such an attractive personality and an effective, courageous leader in the early church. His toughest lesson was that while talented, he could never live out the teaching of Jesus in his own strength. This is great news for the rest of us! We cannot accomplish much for God if we do not venture beyond the limits of our understanding and ability.

The essence of Christianity is simple and practical. It is about people far from God drawing close through the crucified and resurrected Jesus. It is about God's Spirit empowering ordinary people to love, serve, and care for others wherever they live and work. Water stored in a tank is of little use unless it is poured out. Salt in a box preserves nothing, neither does it enhance taste. Christian teaching stored in the head is theoretical abstraction making no difference in the real world.

Community living is where the abstract becomes lived out. Jesus' teaching either works or is dismissed as nonsense. None of us are experts. We are filled with doubts, insecurities, unbelief, and hesitancy. Together we get to encourage one another to take another step in the new, supernatural life as a follower of Jesus. Where we are weak, others are more experienced, and vice versa. Loving one another involves people, forgiving involves people, serving involves people, worship involves people. And it has always been a mixed blessing—in other words, agony and ecstasy.

CONSIDER:

What is your experience with community and relating to other people? Is there scar tissue that causes you to withdraw and protect? Have you been fortunate to belong to a friendly and supportive group? Talk to Jesus about your journey; go for a walk with him and unburden your heart. Listen to his heart. He cares about you in relationship to others because you contribute something precious, and you have gifts to receive that can only be delivered through other people.

GALATIANS 6:1–2

Brothers and sisters, if someone is caught in a sin, you who live by the Spirit should restore that person gently. But watch yourselves, or you also may be tempted. Carry each other's burdens, and in this way you will fulfill the law of Christ.

48 | Three Strings

THIS STORY INVOLVES THE world-famous violinist Itzhak Perlman. Crippled with polio from the age of four, he overcame significant obstacles on his musical journey to achieve international adulation. On one occasion, Perlman had just begun playing a symphony when one of his violin strings snapped. The audience expected him to hobble offstage and find another violin. Instead, he kept playing, ignoring the fact that no one can play a symphony on a violin with three strings. Except that night, he did. The music was beautiful and received a standing ovation. When asked about the incident afterwards, Perlman responded with one sentence: "Our job is to make music with what remains."

It's a universal theme, isn't it? Peter and John—men transformed by their friendship with Jesus—stood before a crippled man at the gate of the temple: "Silver and gold I do not have, but what I do have I give you. In the name of Jesus Christ of Nazareth, walk" (Acts 3:6). Or the little boy handing his meager lunch to Jesus, which became the seed for the miracle of multiplication that would feed more than five thousand people. If his mother had known where his lunch would end up, she'd probably have said, "I'd have packed the best meal I could." Jesus is content with the ordinary and everyday, not our best effort to impress, as if somehow that would make it easier for him to perform a miracle.

Paul talked about learning to be content in all circumstances. It's frighteningly easy to discount ourselves with negative reasoning and defeated conclusions. "If only . . . " is probably on the lips of many of us, leading us to delay or even cancel hopes, dreams, or aspirations. Consider Jesus. If ever anyone played with broken strings, he is surely the greatest virtuoso of all time. God in human form living a life of power, integrity, and love in a fallen, hostile, and rebellious world? Talk about a challenge! On stage with three strings dangling and only one to play on. He made it sound so beautiful that people down the ages have had their lives changed by the symphonic music flowing from his life.

Fortunately, he was not a vain exhibitionist but rather preferred the role of conductor or teacher. He invited everyone he met to join his orchestra, without a thought as to how gifted they were. None of the disciples would have been chosen if the maestro himself had demanded they be experts. As they traveled with Jesus and witnessed what he could do, as they heard the sounds from the life of this extraordinary man, they plucked up the courage to play themselves. Before long, an orchestra of one- or two-stringed instruments, their snapped strings trailing, began to form. Onlookers were amazed. "Look at these people. They are unschooled, ordinary men and women."

That's always been the message of Jesus. But it often gets lost, buried beneath piles of rules, experts, traditions, or spiritual political correctness that stifles rather than blesses the spirit. People looked at the young Itzhak and discounted the brilliance of his playing as a thirteen-year-old boy because of his leg braces and crutches. Not only others, but we ourselves can be wrong about who we are. We tend to focus on the failures or the negatives, the broken strings. It's easy to do. But Jesus always multiplies the one string, or the one sandwich, we offer him. If we give him what we have, and who we are, the miracle will happen. He will make us look extremely gifted and good; he'll applaud from the wings and allow us to receive praise without needing to steal the limelight.

CONSIDER:

Let's resist the easy escape of giving up, blaming something outside ourselves, or concluding, "It will never happen." Naturally, we all have limitations and different skill sets, but supernaturally in God's hands, every one of us can be a source of profoundly beautiful music that will bless and enrich others. They may even say of us, as they said of Jesus, "Isn't that just the carpenter's son/daughter from Nazareth? Look at him/her now. Who would have thought?" Is there a dream that you once had that is not as dead as you might think? If the thought still causes your heart to skip a beat—blow on those embers one more time and let the music flow.

MATTHEW 13:54–55

Coming to his hometown, he began teaching the people in their synagogue, and they were amazed. "Where did this man get this wisdom and these miraculous powers?" they asked. "Isn't this the carpenter's son? Isn't his mother's name Mary, and aren't his brothers James, Joseph, Simon, and Judas?"

Begin to weave and God will give the thread.
GERMAN PROVERB

49 | God's Olympics

CAST YOUR MIND BACK to 2012. The Olympics in London are in their final week, and every day we watch and read accounts of triumph and heartbreak in the race for gold and glory. Some stories are truly inspiring, such as that of the athlete who grew up in Somalia, was abducted to be a child soldier, ran away, and eventually found a home and opportunity in America. There he developed a love for running, and now he stands on the podium, a gold medal draped around his neck.

There's Simon Whitfield from Canada, who slipped on his bike, broke a collarbone, and his four years of training ended in the gutter. Magnificent though the Olympics may be, there are very few winners or those who share the limelight on the podium. This got me thinking about God's Olympic vision and whom he places on podiums and celebrates as winners.

I am reminded of the occasion when Jesus was in the temple and observed people making their offerings. The rich threw in their large contributions, but it was the widow with her two small copper coins who caught his eye and was lifted into the spotlight. Proportionally, she had given more than the rich, who had plenty leftover. Jesus responded with a standing ovation. God's Kingdom on earth as in heaven measures value by kindness of heart; by attitudes that place others first, serve joyfully, and find gold in the satisfaction of being available for Jesus to use.

Followers of Jesus live for an audience of one, and anything else is a bonus. He notices things that we dismiss or attach little significance to. For instance, he admonished the disciples when they tried to keep children away, he stopped on the road for a noisy blind man, he felt the touch of a discouraged and broken woman desperate for physical healing. Jesus spoke about God his Father being aware of the number of hairs on our head. When we offer someone a drink of water, or a helping hand (thinking nobody cares), he is watching. He said it was as if we had had shown that kindness to him.

There is an underlying principle here. To experience the reality of Jesus and the power of his Spirit daily, and have a faith that is vibrant and alive, we must spend less time asking God to do things and focus more on receiving and releasing. Live from that place where we thank him for his love and care, and then be intentional about serving others. The champions in God's Kingdom are not the ones who talk, think, and debate in great forums. They are those who demonstrate love by praying for others, offering to help, being reliable, giving generously of time or substance and expecting nothing in return . . . just like Jesus.

CONSIDER:

Someone said, "I'm a coin in Jesus' pocket to spend however he chooses every day." And a fridge magnet declares, "Dance as if no one's watching." Are you learning to live like that?

MATTHEW 20:16, 26–28

"So the last will be first, and the first will be last . . . whoever wants to become great among you must be your servant, and whoever wants to be first must be your slave—just as the Son of Man did not come to be served, but to serve, and to give his life as a ransom for many.

50 | Hitchhiking

MANY YEARS AGO, I hitchhiked around southern Africa. I traveled fourteen thousand miles from Cape Town to Harare (in Zimbabwe) and was heading south to Swaziland. When I was dropped off at the border crossing, I must have looked suspicious with my wild, long hair and bulging backpack. Everything had to be taken out of my backpack as the guards questioned me about drugs and my activities. With nothing to hide, I came out smelling like a rose. By this time it was late in the afternoon, and I walked down the highway praying for God to get me a lift before dark. Within fifteen minutes a beautiful cream Rolls Royce rolled through the border post. "Lord, it would be cool to have this car stop for me," I whispered as I stuck my thumb out with zero expectancy. Lo and behold, the driver pulled up and offered me a ride all the way to Johannesburg. We stopped at a nearby town where we had dinner together (which he paid for) and stayed overnight before heading out early the next morning.

I learned a lot about trusting God during my days of hitchhiking, when it was the only way I could afford to travel and see the world in the African subcontinent. I slept in a police station one night, a cemetery another, and on a few occasions wondered whether I would ever be picked up. I hated the feeling when the driver pulled over to drop me off and I had to head out into the unknown again. However, my courage soon began to rise as I walked down the highway facing the oncoming traffic, thumb raised expectantly. There is something exhilarating about not knowing how things will work out and stepping into an adventure anyway.

I look back on those days and recall one of my first rides. It was in the small cab of a truck with a load of oranges in the back, driving the winding coastal road in South Africa between the towns of George and Knysna. I was so relieved to be picked up—until the driver pulled out a flask of whisky and sipped on it for the duration of the trip. Fortunately, it was not too long. And in more than ten thousand miles of hitchhiking, that was the only time I felt nervous with a driver.

These moments are metaphors for life and our journey with Jesus. If I'd waited until I could afford to travel, I'd never have left home. Instead, I put together what I could and set out anyway and had some amazing adventures. The same was true when I said "yes" to full-time ministry and found myself studying in Oxford for three years. Or on my return to ministry, when I experienced the Lord providing for all my needs and eventually opening the way for a church to be birthed. Maybe that is why I find it easier to trust God today with my present and future, with my resources or lack thereof? Sometimes we must take risks to know that God is faithful and will never let us go.

We are on an exciting adventure; sometimes we may get a little nervous and even apprehensive. That is why we are learning to talk to one another and encourage each other to believe for what we do not yet see. That is why we expect there to be occasions when we question if we have made the right decision. It is at such times that we are reminded that God our Father loves us and will provide for us, even when we take a wrong turn. It is easy to play it safe in a Bible study or prayer meeting (they are essential of course, you know what I mean); but following Christ is not supposed to be easy. Yes, we may encounter the odd whisky drinker or the inconvenient border patrol search, but that is a small price to pay for driving down the highway in a Rolls Royce, singing, "Thank You, Jesus," with a smile on our face.

Do not wait until you are ready; God is—and that is all that matters.

CONSIDER:

If you were absolutely assured of success, what might you do? What adventure would you love to have? Dream of what you would love to do if it wasn't quite so risky. Why not go for it anyway? Of course, use common sense; before you make a risky decision consult with wise friends and family who know you well. Jumping "in the name of Jesus" is not a licence for silly or dangerous actions.

JOSHUA 1:9

Have I not commanded you? Be strong and courageous. Do not be afraid; do not be discouraged, for the Lord your God will be with you wherever you go.

51 | A Taste of Heaven

When Jesus recounted the story of the prodigal son, he described the Father's house as a venue for joy, dancing, music, and laughter. It sounds like a place brimming with life and great celebration. The only one who did not appreciate the noise spilling out over the fields was a miserable and angry older brother. He disapproved of the grace being demonstrated to "his Father's son."

Here is an invitation and a challenge. How about, as God's sons and daughters, we strive to attain, and model, a taste of heaven on earth? A "taste of heaven" is a real-life encounter with God's love and mercy. It could be receiving a generous gift, being unconditionally forgiven, or not being judged when we expected the worst.

One night, at our local street market, a group of us from church were offering a prayer for healing when a man came by and said he had tennis elbow that had been hurting for quite a while.

"It'll heal naturally," he said.

"Why don't you let us pray for you?" we suggested. "Why wait six months for what could happen now?"

He sat on a chair and shrugged. "If anything happens, I will have to change my way of thinking."

Four of us knelt and prayed, and three minutes later when asked how his elbow felt he replied, "That's amazing, it really is more than 50 percent better!" We prayed some more, and he left shaking his head in wonder. It was a long, slow evening out there on the street, but hairline cracks of breakthrough are to be celebrated.

The reason believers in Jesus declare God's praises and encourage an expression of vocal thanksgiving is because we seem to have forgotten how to express ourselves freely. We in church have become so serious and easily offended by emotions. It is perhaps good for us to ask ourselves why. Joyful celebration is a hallmark of God's presence.

Joy is not the same as happiness, which comes and goes. Joy is rooted in God's faithfulness that never changes. He is the same yesterday, today, forever. Joy is a declaration that God's love for me is assured, that he is Lord over every situation and circumstance. Because of his promises, we can have hope, even in the darkest of times. And on those occasions when we may feel discouraged, it is helpful to speak out a greater truth rooted in God's love that is stronger than our present emotions.

CONSIDER:

How do you experience joy? Do circumstances determine joy for you, or does it bubble up from the inside? Perhaps a combination? Are you growing in freedom in expressing emotion in the presence of others, or have you withdrawn and declared that you are "not like that"? Talk to Jesus about your responses. How would you feel if he embraced you?

JOHN 14:13–14

And I will do whatever you ask in my name, so that the Father may be glorified in the Son. You may ask me for anything in my name, and I will do it.

52 | Joy

When I lose joy (see Musing 51) I know for sure that hope is low. My moods tend to be darker, and I can be irritable and impatient. When joy and hope are distant, my faith in God's goodness is encrusted with barnacles of frustration, probably disillusionment, and a sense of merely surviving and being self-reliant. Much of what robs me of joy and hope is rooted in circumstances and/or the impact of others around me. This can be further compounded by the negative inner dialogue that can chatter away forever if given free reign. Having lived in that joyless place without hope for years (and fought through it), it is not somewhere I desire to return to if I can avoid it.

At a prayer time recently, someone remarked, "If God is humble, then why would he want us to praise him rather than serve him quietly and humbly?" That is a good question echoed by many, including me years ago when it seemed to me God had an ego problem. Why would he need us to applaud him and tell him how wonderful he is? Fortunately, there was someone to answer my question and explain that joy and worship have nothing to do with God's ego. He does not need my response to fulfil himself; he is secure and complete in his identity without needing our praise to complete him or provide reassurance. Worship is for our benefit. We need our response to be expressed for *us* to be fulfilled.

It is like when, standing at the rim of the Grand Canyon, seeing the magnificent sight before me, I cannot help but exclaim, "Wow, that's amazing, breathtaking, so beautiful!" I take out my camera and snap photographs to show others; I update my status on Facebook with a picture of "me at the Grand Canyon." My response to the beauty I see is evoked and rises spontaneously from within me—quite unrehearsed. I enjoy how I feel as I respond; it revives and refreshes me.

That is what God desires for us when believers gather: to come alive and be refreshed! It would be grossly unfair and insensitive to expect a blind person to rejoice at the beauty of the Grand Canyon; however, if we could restore their sight, then all would be changed. We too can ask God to heal and release us where we feel unable, blind, or paralyzed. Rather than defensively justifying my lack, I would rather ask for more joy and hope so that my cup is spilling out, splashing good things over others. And I have learned that Jesus is the source from which everything flows, and overflows.

Stand in front of a mirror and make faces: see yourself scowling, expressionless, and then smiling. Which do you think is most appealing? It's that simple! When I lack joy or hope I can either become angry reading this kind of musing, or I can recognize my lack thereof and simply ask God to help me know him and see him more clearly, so that I too can experience more of his joy.

CONSIDER:

What is getting in the way of more joy in your life? Are God's promises and the declarations above in these verses not enough to counter the challenges? Would you trust the promises of a person who cannot lie, who always has your best interest at heart, and who has the power to inspire and change any circumstance? That is God.

Did you know that the command to "rejoice" or "be joyful" occurs seventy-two times in the New Testament? Seventy-two times we Christians are told to be joyful. Joy is to be one of our defining characteristics. Here are some verses to inspire and encourage.

PHILIPPIANS 4:4

Rejoice in the Lord always. I will say it again: Rejoice!

ROMANS 14:17

For the kingdom of God is not a matter of eating and drinking, but of righteousness, peace, and joy in the Holy Spirit . . .

JOHN 7:37–38

On the last and greatest day of the festival, Jesus stood and said in a loud voice, "Let anyone who is thirsty come to me and drink. Whoever believes in me, as Scripture has said, rivers of living water will flow from within them."

1 PETER 1:8–9

Though you have not seen him, you love him; and even though you do not see him now, you believe in him and are filled with an inexpressible and glorious joy, for you are receiving the result of your faith, the salvation of your souls.

Father, may all who read this know a greater measure of joy rising up from within, AMEN!

*Good advice is often annoying;
bad advice never is.*

FRENCH PROVERB

53 | Orphans No Longer

A FEW YEARS AGO, I visited an orphanage in Uganda. I was accompanying Pat, a stoic lady from my church who had established this refuge for street orphans.

It was nearly ten o'clock at night when the bus rattled and rolled into Mbarara (north of Kampala). It carefully idled down one more eroded street to the compound where the boys lived. I am ashamed to admit that I was frustrated and weary after what should have been a four-hour trip had stretched into seven and a half hours of extreme endurance.

The boys were delighted to greet us, chattering and bouncing around; they had not seen their beloved Pat for six months. I was proudly shown to my room—a grimy concrete square with a hideous pink mosquito net draped above a single bed. A square of linoleum covered one third of the concrete floor. In one corner, a noisy freezer that had seen better days sounded as if it were chewing ice. A small bookshelf with a few plates behind a curtain completed the furnishings. Tastefully placed beside the bed, a can of Raid hinted at the presence of a few nocturnal visitors. A well-used plastered tool shed had been cleaned out and painted with watered-down white paint. It was completely empty and was proudly presented to me as my private washing area, complete with a blue plastic basin and a new sponge. The toilet was a small concrete room with a square opening in the floor over which all ablutions were conducted in a squatting position. Three stood side by side—two for the boys and one for me.

"From Vancouver to this . . . " I muttered to myself behind a polite smile of diluted gratitude. I was tired and wanted to retreat into my own company. But I was not alone. As I reflected on the frustrating and uncomfortable journey, and the threadbare facilities, the voice of God whispered to my spirit, "What did you expect? What you experience as the bottom of the pit is a step up for these boys. This filthy compound represents hope, love, food, and a home they have never known. Besides, what do you think I did for you?"

It didn't take me long to feel as if I'd been there for months. On the second evening, the goat that greeted me with wide-eyed curiosity on my arrival was roasting on a coal fire, her head lying in the grass somewhat detached. The night before I returned to Canada, the boys dressed in various costumes, danced, and pounded drums in the courtyard outside, shouting with delight. Later we crowded into a small room and sang songs and talked about God. The boys smiled and laughed during the music, and when we thought of the love of the Father there was a deep silence. They had so little. Pat had found most of them on the streets without a home, their parents dead from HIV, or in some cases they were fleeing from a bad situation.

Many recounted how they drank at night because it "helped me sleep"—and they were younger than twelve years old! Part of me wanted to stay and help build this very humble community and be a father to them. But I had my own family waiting back home. One young boy shyly knocked on my door and asked me to pray for him—he had kidney disease and a slightly deformed leg. We chatted for a while before I laid hands on him and prayed for the love and power of God to touch him: "Let your Kingdom come, Lord, on earth as in heaven." I later learned that his kidney was healed. Jesus loves everyone without exception, and journeys anywhere, and everywhere. Rejoice, Immanuel—God is with us!

CONSIDER:

What are you dissatisfied with? What if God is offering you contentment today, even when everything is not perfect? How about spending time today reflecting on what you have, appreciating, giving thanks, and even sharing what you long for with God—your kind, interested, attentive, and caring Father.

PHILIPPIANS 4:12

I know what it is to be in need, and I know what it is to have plenty. I have learned the secret of being content in any and every situation, whether well fed or hungry, whether living in plenty or in want.

54 | God's Spirit in Us

"Stretch out your hand to heal and perform signs and wonders through the name of your holy servant Jesus!" (Acts 4:30). The day before praying these words, Peter and John healed a crippled man at the gate of the temple. The fallout, from the man, was dancing and joy; but church leadership directed angry threats at Peter and John.

Peter stood up in the marketplace to explain what had happened. He identified the resurrected Jesus Christ as the only one capable of performing such a wonder through them. He and John were dragged before religious leaders, to whom he gave the same defense, only to be thrown in jail for the night. Frustrated, the leaders eventually let them go. They returned to their friends and raised their voices to heaven, requesting even more power be released through them.

In the years they spent following Jesus, the disciples learned something fundamental to Christianity. It was what made Jesus so appealing to the same people the religious leaders could neither impress nor attract. Jesus introduced people to the love of God AND to his power. Why was that so appealing to the masses? Because all their lives they had been talked down to by spiritual leaders—told what to think, how to behave, what pleased God, and how many sacrifices were acceptable. It was a never-ending circuit of things they had to do to remain in good standing with God.

Their personal well-being was never a topic of conversation, and if they were suffering in any way, they were more likely to be judged or cast out than helped. After all, they deserved it; they had sinned. Little wonder that, when Jesus stepped into their world, the common man and woman were astonished at the wisdom that came from his mouth, the kindness and love that shone through his eyes, and the power of heaven that was released through his words and touch. They had never experienced anything like what Jesus revealed.

Imagine encountering God and discovering that he is willing and able to heal your disease; that he is gentle and kind, and he treats you and your friends as if you are important! That is what the disciples learned. Therefore, when they went out into the marketplace with the Holy Spirit alive within them, they expected power to flow through them and bless and release everyone they encountered.

God's Spirit can be likened to a strong rushing river with healing along its shores wherever it flows—available at any time. When there is no river, the church retreats behind its walls and becomes merely a religious institution—a dry riverbed with only a trickle of a stream. Everything atrophies back to the human comfort zone of ritual and lecture, insiders and outsiders, us and them.

In every local church we still have much to learn and grow into. We do know that we are called to be "river people." Venturing out into the marketplace is going to become increasingly normal. The focus of ministry is prophetic, which means learning to listen to God and to speak encouragement over people in order that they may dare to believe that God is good and loves them specifically.

Those early disciples were unschooled, ordinary people who'd spent time with Jesus. Three years in the presence of Jesus made all the difference in the world. We are living in times where *all that is required* for us to witness God's power and prophetic words flowing through us into the world is a willingness to receive God's love in Jesus and give it away. It takes practice, humility, being teachable, and the desire to be more than one who merely "believes" in God.

CONSIDER:

Do not miss the opportunity to be a part of something wonderful for God. Imagine Jesus using you to enable a cripple to dance in the streets. Why not? Unbelievable? That is a good start. Then, dare to pray for someone with a cold, or a headache, or a bad mood.

This is my prayer for you:

I thank God for you.

For all the love you give others, seen and unseen.
For all the grace, mercy, and hope you demonstrate to those around you.
For his plans for you to be a witness and to find joy in that.
I thank God for you, that you may be his light to those around you.

COLOSSIANS 1:29

To this end I strenuously contend with all the energy Christ so powerfully works in me.

> *Shared joy is a double joy;*
> *shared sorrow is half a sorrow.*
>
> SWEDISH PROVERB

55 | Declarations amid Despair

I fumbled through books, desperately scanning pages for a glimmer of light to pierce through the dark cavern of my mind. Depression gripped me in its jaws like a crocodile snatches its victim and, writhing, drags it into the depths. I felt helpless. I could see no way of escape, no end in sight.

I was reading the writings of those who had endured depression; how were they still alive? I was so devoid of hope that even knowing the authors survived made a difference.

Years later, I reflect on that dark time, astounded at what transpired. It was only God, in his mercy and grace, who rescued me from what felt quite literally like the jaws of death. Once one has trudged through the valley of the shadow of death, when hope rises like a dawning sun, above a horizon you thought was lost, you never want to lose sight of it again.

I realize now that much of my life, my joy, my hope, and even my faith had been stolen by a cunning thief who aims to kill and destroy. Call him satan, call him the devil, call him evil or whatever you want. You may not believe in him, but he believes in you as a host for the parasite he is. I had allowed him to gain access by my poor choices rooted in my circumstances. Believing lies, I had been reduced to a weak and pathetic victim. But because I am writing this, you know it was not the end; God does redeem and help us overcome.

I listened to a talk recently which reminded me that the only living "being" to whom God has given legitimate authority is humans—you and me—made in his image. That authority is to be exercised over the earth and all living creatures, not over one another. Evil has no authority at all other than that which we relinquish to it.

Like a vampire, it feeds off those who lose their identity as sons and daughters of the living God. It diminishes them to ineffective skeletons far removed from the vibrant people the Father intends them to be. As an emaciated body reveals disease or starvation, so too a person lacking identity or God's Spirit within them is lifeless, without hope. But . . .

God releases hope and joy among his people that grows from the depths of who he is for us—and in us. It is neither superficial nor naive but is the fruit of a confidence we have in his faithfulness, his goodness, and his promise to never leave us or forsake us. It is hope in the heart, where the blood flows; it is not nourished by intellectual concepts. It is born from the love of the Father revealed through his Son, Jesus, and brought to life in us by his Spirit.

The mandate for any Christian community is to be a place where heaven touches earth, releasing hope and joy into the world—even where circumstances and situations are tough. Declarations of God's goodness are powerful. Yes, when one is overwhelmed by dark despair they can sound pathetic and irritating. But speaking truth to darkness weakens its grip. For instance: "I am deeply loved. God is with me now. He is not angry, and he cares about my situation. He holds me close right now, even when I feel nothing. I believe he will help me through this, step by step, day by day."

I know what unbelief and anger feel like firsthand. Affirming revelations and declarations saved my life and helped me find hope for a future I never believed possible. Unfortunately, most of us know the real power in darkness and negativity, often more than we experience the much, much more that is offered and unleashed through hope in Jesus.

Christianity is meant to be powerful and life-changing! My joyful testimony now is that I find it hard to comprehend the years when I felt so trapped and hopeless. God has no favorites, and these declarations need to be spoken out as we choose to rise and take hold of our life and destiny. Attitudes and habits such as criticism, negativity, pessimism, and depression can be as familiar as old friends, sticking like barnacles to our spirits. Begin to soak them in declarations and they will, much to your surprise, drop off as hope reclaims the ground that has been stolen from you.

CONSIDER:

What phrases run through your head about yourself that are negative and lies? Write them down, cross them out, and then write down what Jesus would say instead. If you find it difficult to talk to yourself, pretend you are speaking to a friend.

Psalm 40:1–3

I waited patiently for the Lord; he turned to me and heard my cry. He lifted me out of the slimy pit, out of the mud and mire; he set my feet on a rock and gave me a firm place to stand. He put a new song in my mouth, a hymn of praise to our God. Many will see and fear the Lord and put their trust in him.

56 | More Than Able

It was an ordinary day in the wilderness a few miles from the Dead Sea. In the shadow of the imposing mountain with a fortress on top called Masada, a young goat herder was hungry. He wanted to get home before sunset and was gathering the goats. One of them had wandered into a cave. He whistled and shouted but the animal failed to appear, so he threw a rock into the darkness. To his surprise, he heard the clatter of breaking pottery. Forgetting about the goat, he ventured further inside to investigate. Hidden in the cool shadows he discovered large jars containing what looked like old leather. He removed a few pieces, found his goat, and headed home.

In the months that followed, he returned to the cave for more pieces, coaxed by his uncle who had fashioned them into fine sandals. That is, until another relative suggested the material he was using may be more than "old leather." He visited another friend, who passed on a fragment, and as the word spread huge excitement built. The cave was visited by experts, and the announcement of the discovery of the Dead Sea Scrolls hit the headlines around the world. These were ancient manuscripts of the Old Testament and other writings, including the book of Isaiah—one thousand years older than anything ever seen before. What someone thought was old leather another identified as a priceless manuscript containing a portion of the word of God.

One never knows how and when the supernatural will break into an everyday moment. It is an exciting prospect to consider: how many "words of God" in our lives have we missed because we thought we were handling something ordinary, mundane, or old? When we keep company with Jesus for any length of time and allow him some measure of freedom, we will discover that we are involved in an adventure, the likes of which we have never known before. There's so much more to God than merely believing a few doctrines and attending a Sunday service!

The disciples were attracted to Jesus precisely because he was unlike anyone they had ever met. He lifted their lives and experiences from the predictable to the extraordinary, day after day: water into wine, loaves and fishes multiplied, healing after healing, walking on water, calming a storm, casting out demons, and rising from the dead. Paul became a Christian because of a supernatural encounter on the Damascus Road that left this forceful intellectual zealot blind and speechless. Three days later, he was convinced that Jesus, the one whom he despised, was indeed the risen Son of God—a revelation that took years to piece together. His life and mission turned in an entirely different direction, one that the previous week would have been unthinkable for him and his contemporaries.

Many years later, Paul wrote to the Ephesians words rooted in experience and future promise: "Now to him who is able to do immeasurably more than all we ask or imagine, according to his power that is at work within us . . . " (Ephesians 3:20). That prayer was forged in a long life experiencing firsthand the faithful provision of God through many incredibly difficult circumstances—more than he could ask or imagine.

CONSIDER:

Jesus seldom does anything without an invitation. He is always willing to answer, guide, encourage, comfort, and lead. Ask him for faith to believe for more, eyes to see, and ears to hear him. And if you have never invited him into your heart, now would be a great time.

REVELATION 3:20

Here I am! I stand at the door and knock. If anyone hears my voice and opens the door, I will come in and eat with that person, and they with me.

57 | Forty Days

Ash Wednesday marks the beginning of forty days of Lent. The practice began early in church history, as a shorter, three-day period of fasting for personal reflection and penance as Easter approached. Later, around AD 600, it was stretched to forty days—probably modeled on Jesus fasting in the wilderness for forty days before beginning his public ministry. Throughout my childhood and teenage years, Lent was observed in the Anglican school I attended and continues to be very much part of Protestant and Catholic liturgical practice today. As I have grown older, I've questioned the value and ultimate purpose of this tradition. Is it merely a self-imposed religious burden or an anointed gift from God?

I am sure God will bless any person who comes to him with a humble heart whether observing Lent or not. As a teenager I recall occasions when I tried to enter the meaning of Lent and "give up something I liked" for forty days. I cannot remember the impact on my spiritual life, but I suspect it reinforced an understanding of God who is to be revered and feared more than embraced and loved. Furthermore, it drew attention yet again to my identity as a sinner who must try to earn his way into the presence of almighty God—if I can only be disciplined, good, and obedient enough. That is why I have concluded that it is a religious act better left in Egypt than carried into the Promised Land (certainly for new believers).

Egyptian Christianity focuses on our present identity as slaves to sin, God forgiving us through the blood of the Lamb/Jesus on the cross, and one day being free—when we get to heaven. Until then we have "salvation through Jesus" in terms of being forgiven and saved from hell, our focus on earth being to keep the Ten Commandments and live good Christian lives. God is still distant, Jesus is a great role model and example, and the Bible is the handbook outlining God's expectations, standards, and rules.

The Christian experience is one of attendance at church, Bible study, serving others, and being careful not to be influenced by the wayward misguided thoughts and lifestyles of non-believers. Many Christians who live in this camp are sincere, earnest, hard-working, faithful believers. They have never been told that heaven begins now, and freedom is closer than they know.

The irony is that it is precisely because of what Jesus accomplished on the cross and resurrection that we (human beings) do not need to add our personal sacrificial touches to earn acceptance; sacrifice as a fruit of love is what we are called to. Jesus' stunning crucified life reconciles everyone who recognizes his sacrifice to God and draws them into his embrace. There is nothing more we can add to earn reconciliation other than to say, "thank you" and walk into the Father's outstretched arms. This is amazing grace at work, reaching into the human heart, reconciling one who was lost, and inviting them into a new life they never dreamed possible.

Imagine if instead of forty days of Lent we celebrated a Christian version of forty days of thanks and praise—God's outrageous love poured out in random acts of kindness by those who profess to follow Jesus. Imagine forty days of celebration, healing, and festivities declaring the revelation of what has been made possible to all with such freedom and passion! What image of God would be shared with the world, and how might they respond to love and joy, generosity and laughter?

There is no doubt that times of reflection and a sober appreciation of Jesus' sacrifice are necessary. The trouble is that many people I meet have overdosed on that message. They have seldom, if ever, tasted and seen the depth and breadth of his love offered to every living soul. I encourage you to celebrate Lent from the Promised Land perspective.

CONSIDER:

Enter your relationship with God your Father with joy; do something that will foster and nurture your relationship. Perhaps it is reading the Bible more often, or daring to participate in worship with greater passion, maybe attending a teaching session or prayer time that you do not normally venture out to. You could be risky and ask Jesus to give you opportunities to share your relationship with him with a friend. There are many creative ways to take responsibility for building and exercising your faith from the inside out. Do it with a smile and with joy; and if you want to eat fish on Friday, that is fine.

Matthew 11:17–19

"'We played the pipe for you,
 and you did not dance;
we sang a dirge,
 and you did not mourn.'

For John came neither eating nor drinking, and they say, 'He has a demon.' The Son of Man came eating and drinking, and they say, 'Here is a glutton and a drunkard, a friend of tax collectors and sinners.' But wisdom is proved right by her deeds."

58 | Like a Lion

THE LION, WITHOUT QUESTION, is a symbol of majesty, power, royalty, and strength. In the wild the male lion roars as a sign of authority and to protect his territory—that roar can be heard up to five miles away. When it comes to hunting, the lioness is the primary participant; after making the kill, the male lion has first access to the spoils. We are familiar with Jesus portrayed in the Bible as a roaring lion ("Lion of Judah" in Revelation 5:5; Hosea 11:10).

While Jesus is the Lion King, the church is usually described as the "Bride of Christ." However, in the metaphor that portrays Jesus as a lion, it is interesting to consider the church as a lioness, active and hunting while the Lion King roars and defends the wider territory. I love the revelation that transforms us into those who engage in battle rather than passively waiting for God to do everything for us; of people who initiate and take risks to reach others who have never known the love of the Father or his presence. We are highlighting one aspect of who God is, as on other occasions he is called "the Lamb."

What is God teaching us? He is saying that he roared when the earth was created, when Jesus walked this earth, when he was crucified, resurrected, and when his Spirit was poured out on all flesh. And that he continues to roar, declaring his authority and ultimate dominion over all the earth. It is useless for the lioness to constantly pray for him to hunt when that task has been delegated to her. It is an act of disobedience for the lioness to be passive or to neglect to teach her young how to fend for themselves. All the while, the male lion watches over them and ensures the territory is secure, in which they will play their part.

The analogy changes with a little imagination. Instead of a lioness out on the hunt to kill the weak, Christians are commissioned and expected to be on the hunt for the weak and the lost to offer healing and a welcome home. The pride of lions never expects an animal to wander into their presence. Neither should believers assume that all they are called to do is sit with closed eyes and ask God to do everything required for their happiness on earth. Lion cubs grow into adults. We who follow Jesus are destined to become heralds, warriors, healers, light, and salt in a dark and tasteless world. This is not brash bravado or empty rhetoric. It is what Jesus went to the cross to accomplish—a future for God's lost and broken people. Everyone qualifies and is invited to participate.

Those who participate, grow. It is exciting to be covered by the roar of the Lion King, and an incredible privilege to go hunting together. Do not be left behind.

CONSIDER:

Where could you be bolder? What if the Lion King has your back? Create your own adventure with him, step out; he doesn't fuss over which foot comes first, or where. He is not interested in perfection but encourages us to try.

ISAIAH 41:10

"So do not fear, for I am with you; do not be dismayed, for I am your God. I will strengthen you and help you; I will uphold you with my righteous right hand."

59 | Pilgrimage

During summer, driving the highway on Vancouver Island is like joining the camel train to the West Coast, except instead of camels there are all modes of transport wending their way through the famous old growth of Cathedral Grove. Some have motorbikes strapped with gear; others are rented campers ablaze with stunning photographs of scenic Canada, and the largest of course are the motorhomes, loaded with all the comforts of home.

As it is in many places, summer in Canada is the time to hit the road and travel beyond the horizon; to see and experience new things with friends and family. For most, it is an opportunity for a change of pace—to escape the mundane, at least for a few weeks.

Psalm 84 was written for pilgrims on the road to Jerusalem who were fulfilling a lifelong dream to worship God in the temple. This was the holiest place on earth (it still is for devout Jews), where God's presence touched earth in the Holy of Holies and where believers could draw close to him. The writer describes believers worshiping God, hungry for him: "My soul yearns, even faints, for the courts of the Lord; My heart and flesh cry out for the living God" (verse 2). The opportunity to come close to his presence was a big deal and would not be something they could enjoy very often.

This psalm contains a tension—the presence of the Lord in the temple and journeying through the Valley of Baca to get there. It was a valley of drought, thorns, and suffering that most pilgrims had to navigate on their way to Jerusalem. It seems that God's presence and experiencing hardship are inevitable components of life. The psalmist declares with joyful assurance, "Blessed are those whose strength is in you, whose hearts are set on pilgrimage" (verse 5). Hearts set on pilgrimage is the key to life.

Pilgrimage is a lifestyle (rather like lifelong learning). Spiritually adventurous lives are constantly on the move. How is that possible without becoming travel-jaded and weary with motion sickness? Jesus spent much of his public life on the road, always appearing to be comfortable, at peace, and at home wherever he was. He was sustained by the company he kept as he traveled. He was aware all day and night of not being alone. He listened to his Father's voice, spent time alone with him in the hills, and was vulnerably dependent upon the power of the Spirit within him to perform miracles.

Everyone around Jesus was looking for peace, happiness, and provision in things, places, people, or even journeys to Jerusalem. Jesus, never being selfish or proud, wanted to share the secret. "The kingdom of God is within you," he told them (Luke 17:21). At that time no one understood that he was preparing the way for the revolutionary gift of God the Father's presence within—to be released over all humanity.

In Jesus, the home of God the Father is moving into the hearts of people who welcome him. Human beings (God's temple) are to be the dwelling place of God's Spirit—on earth as in heaven—as was the case with Adam before the fall. During Jesus' unique life, death, and resurrection, the curtain in the temple of Jerusalem was torn in two. The Spirit of God escaped from such a restricted place of presence, destroying the fantasy that God could be packaged in a box crafted from human hands. After the resurrection, the Spirit of God was at long last able to return "home"—to be present within every person willing to bow humbly to Jesus.

CONSIDER:

How aware are you that God's life and Spirit have made their home within you? Have you invited him to dwell within you? If not, would you like to? He is more than willing. "Come Holy Spirit, I welcome you into my heart to empower me with the love and presence of Jesus. Thank you." Now, live from that place of acceptance instead of striving. He never leaves home without you!

Psalm 84:5

Blessed are those whose strength is in you, whose hearts are set on pilgrimage.

60 | God with Us

THE IMPLICATIONS OF WHAT we read in Musing 59 are enormous. It is no longer necessary to journey to the temple in Jerusalem to experience God's presence. Jesus' sacrifice and resurrection have broken the barrier between God and humanity. The Father's heart is now permanently accessible to every son and daughter on earth as in heaven, which means he is present wherever we are! "We" means every person on earth because he is always searching, waiting, wanting to respond to everyone and anyone.

Instead of us journeying through the Valley of Baca to get to him (enduring many struggles along the way), he is already with us. He initiated the journey to draw us close. As the psalmist describes in Psalm 84, we can experience God our Father transforming deserts and places of struggle into wells of living water. I will never forget young goat herders outside Jerusalem leading me and my traveling companions through rocky terrain. Sliding aside a large stone, they exposed a huge natural well of crystal-clear cold water below the surface and offered us a drink: "Taste and see!" On our own, my friends and I would never have found it.

It is good news for those of us constantly wanting to get away from it all, yearning for a time in the future when we do not have to deal with whatever our life is now. Jesus won for us the joy and encouragement of knowing the presence of his family wherever we happen to be—every day and night of our lives. It is as if we are traveling in a large motorhome with all the resources of heaven at our disposal. The only difference is that this is spiritual, which means that as we allow God to speak to us on the inside, he brings about transformation on the outside. He shows us wells we would never have uncovered without him.

If you sometimes are envious of those big motorhomes the size of buses with a utility vehicle in tow and wish you were part of that entourage—don't be. It is expensive and exhausting traveling the world looking for peace and happiness. If that were the only way to possess the things you long for, then those priceless gifts would be accessible to about 1 percent of the world's population. But God does not play favorites. Instead, it is all gifted to anyone who asks the Father. He loves and adores you, and desires that every day of your life is filled with experiences of his presence and sustenance. It is called "abiding in him."

Listen to promises Jesus makes to you personally:

John 15:7 "If you remain in me and my words remain in you, ask whatever you wish, and it will be done for you."

John 14:18 "I will not leave you as orphans; I will come to you."

John 14:23 "Anyone who loves me will obey my teaching. My Father will love them, and we will come to them and make our home with them."

Hebrews 13:5 "Never will I leave you; never will I forsake you."

All the treasures of heaven are accessed by faith through Jesus by keeping company with him, paid for through the cross and delivered to God's mailbox within you—your heart. That is the only way everyone is included, whether rich or poor, weak or strong, or whatever their circumstances. That is why the gift also comes with a warning as we journey through life.

CONSIDER:

May you know the joy of one whose heart is set on pilgrimage. May the Father who is by your side show you some deep wells to be refreshed from, which you would never have seen or tasted without his presence.

Matthew 6:19–21

"Do not store up for yourselves treasures on earth, where moths and vermin destroy, and where thieves break in and steal. But store up for yourselves treasure in heaven, where moths and vermin do not destroy and where thieves do not break in and steal. For where your treasure is, there your heart will be also."

61 | Extraordinary Wrapped in Ordinary

IMAGINE YOU HAD CREATED a beautiful house and gardens to give to your children, whom you loved with passion. You left them with plenty of resources and instructions to take care of one another and their home. But twenty years later, you returned to find them fighting among each other, the house that you had so lovingly prepared for them in ruins, the furniture broken, the garden overgrown . . .

Your kids were not happy to see you. They did not run to greet you; instead, they virtually ignored you, averting their eyes whenever you looked at them. But you lived among them anyway to awaken at least the possibility of restoring your relationship and the house you built for them. Eventually, tensions reached boiling point and you—the owner, creator, provider, and blood relative—were brutally rejected and killed. Not only that, but you rose again so that you could be there for the same children when they came to the realization of who you were and what they had done.

Christmas is a deep revelation of the humility and sacrificial love of God—a love that is unique, unparalleled in any other faith on earth at any time in history. If we can grab hold of this truth with our hearts and hands, Father Christmas, for many the star of the show, will be reduced to a small part player. Brightly wrapped gifts under the tree become reminders of a greater gift that can never be repaid. The festive season of joy and peace will stretch beyond the Christmas season and begin to define our lives all year round.

When we read history, God invariably appears in the unexpected and is seldom recognized. It is why we encourage one another to pay attention to the daily "ordinary," because therein lie the seeds of the extraordinary—heaven breaking through on earth. Everything we do has the potential to bless others and release transformation in ourselves. We learn to live in joy and peace no matter what our circumstances are, because we know the heart of the Father toward us and embrace it.

We can all benefit from encouragement and teaching about how to step into God's purposes for us individually and as community. The principle is simple and clear. If we want to arrive at the mountaintop, we need to take life one step at a time. It is not earth-shattering, but as a follower of Jesus you can have confidence that steps today are preparing for possible leaps tomorrow. So, what does that look like? It means taking hold of every opportunity that comes our way, no matter how small, because in humble packages we discover the gifts to strengthen and grow us for the steps to follow.

Character is always at the core of the Father's heart for us. There are no shortcuts to those truths embedding in our hearts and eventually becoming part of our nature. Be expectant. Believe that God's hand is upon you at this very moment. There is often more going on than we realize. Mary was just an ordinary young teenager when she became the mother of Jesus. She had no clue about all that was happening with her. Joseph was a carpenter trying to care for a new family after having his life turned upside down with the news of Mary's unexpected pregnancy. Anyone else involved in that first Christmas was going about their daily life quite oblivious to the magnitude of events unfolding around them.

It will be a happy Christmas (and indeed every day) if you and I make room in our hearts for the King of Kings. Then, see what happens as he moves in us and through us to take us places we never imagined possible.

CONSIDER:

What can you do or take hold of today that may nurture the seeds for tomorrow? And on the other end of the scale, dream big and dare to imagine what is possible if you allow the joy and mystery of Jesus to take root in your heart. As you walk through today, can you identify things that are building your character? How could those qualities be preparing you for the future? Trust God with the little details and dream big without trying to work out how.

2 KINGS 6:16–17

"Don't be afraid," the prophet answered. "Those who are with us are more than those who are with them."

And Elisha prayed, "Open his eyes, Lord, so that he may see." Then the Lord opened the servant's eyes, and he looked and saw the hills full of horses and chariots of fire all around Elisha.

Evil enters like a needle and spreads like an oak tree.

ETHIOPIAN PROVERB

62 | Following Jesus

How would you answer the question, "What's it like to believe in Jesus and to follow him?"

For many, many years I struggled to give a clear answer. Probably much of my response would have been a doctrinal statement. You know, something about Jesus, the Son of God, and a bunch of stuff that would probably be true but not captivating to the person asking the question. Here is an answer from an unknown author that I was reminded of recently. It packs some punch and would be a good starting point for all followers of Jesus. See what you think.

"My calling is sure. My challenge is big. My vision is clear. My desire is strong. My influence is eternal. My impact is critical. My values are solid. My faith is tough. My mission is urgent. My purpose is unmistakable. My direction is forward. My heart is genuine. My strength is supernatural. My reward is promised. And my God is real. I refuse to be dismayed, disengaged, disgruntled, discouraged, or distracted. Neither will I look back, stand back, fall back, go back, or sit back. I do not need applause, flattery, adulation, prestige, stature, or veneration. I have no time for business as usual, mediocre standards, small thinking, normal expectations, average results, ordinary ideas, petty disputes, or low vision. I will not give up, give in, bail out, lie down, turn over, quit, or surrender. I am a minister. That is what I do."

When I first read the statement, it impressed me with its boldness and confidence and sense of assuredness. Now, as I review it, that impression lingers, but the pronouns "my" and "I" loom exceptionally large. I know what the person is trying to say. It reminds me of Peter declaring to Jesus that he was the man to be trusted: "I'll never leave you or forsake you!" Then Peter denies Jesus and fails to live up to his sincere declaration.

How would I answer the question? I'd start by changing the pronouns to reflect Jesus' point of view and then read the entire declaration above inserting "his" and "he." When I do that, I am getting close to describing the relationship I'm growing into with Jesus—a relationship where *his* strength and faithfulness are what I depend upon.

That means declaring his love as unconditional, and his mercy and forgiveness as gifts without price wrapped in grace. It means passionately declaring the power of Jesus to heal; how unbelievable it is to walk by his side. He provides a new identity, empowering every follower to release his love through the many cracks of their imperfect lives. Somehow, he manages to transform old wounds and scars into badges of honor that draw attention away from failure and bring the spotlight to rest on his amazing kindness and faithfulness. Best of all, he invites every follower to "show and tell" with him. He gives permission for them to boast about him to others and then invites them to "taste and see" for themselves.

Whereas once perhaps we merely talked about beliefs, we are now free to share his presence and facilitate a personal encounter. We no longer spend much time grappling with intellectual arguments; rather, we declare the goodness of God the Father's heart and his love for the one with whom we are conversing. We illustrate what he has done in our brokenness, rather than telling people what they must do. We get a thrill out of daring them to give him a chance to show how real and personal he is.

I am still blown away when he does just that, or I see someone else's life explode like fireworks in wonderful ways. Jesus has totally touched and changed my life—more than once. He is indeed worthy of all praise!

CONSIDER:

When talking about your faith, do not agonize over your answer, searching for elevated language; ask for passion and experience, and the rest will flow! Tell the stories of how Jesus has impacted your life so far. It does not have to be exaggerated; the humble, quiet, and ordinary can be earth-shattering.

1 CORINTHIANS 1:26–27

Brothers and sisters, think of what you were when you were called. Not many of you were wise by human standards; not many were influential; not many were of noble birth. But God chose the foolish things of the world to shame the wise; God chose the weak things of the world to shame the strong.

63 | Advent

No one knew too clearly what was happening as the events surrounding the first Christmas unfolded. To be honest, it looked like poor planning when Mary and Joseph arrived in Bethlehem. You can imagine their thoughts: *God wants us to carry his Son and can't even arrange for a hotel to have a vacancy?* Eventually, space was found with donkeys and hay in a stable with manure carpeting the floor, mice and rats running the gauntlet, scrounging for a morsel to eat. No matter that the Bread of Life was about to be delivered and would grow to challenge, anger, and save a people (like us perhaps, and many down the ages) who insist on rebaking him every year as a cookie-cutter gingerbread baby. Keep him harmless, a baby, weak and under our control.

Shepherds came to visit, stinking of sheep and caked in mud. They had been invited by an angel appearing to them in the fields. Who would have thought they would be at the top of the guest list? Except, of course, it makes sense when we remember that God has a special affinity for shepherds and identified with them. Maybe God the Father was so moved at the birth of his Son in human form that he wanted someone to kneel by that manger as he would have loved to do. His heart was swelling with incredible emotions of longing, tenderness, and perhaps even trepidation as he thought of what lay ahead for his baby boy. What father would not want to hold and cradle a son or daughter close to his chest and whisper words of love into newly formed ears, promising that he'd never let him go?

Winding their way through the dangerous threats of Herod, the Wise Men journeyed from foreign lands. They had followed a star for weeks to this place in Bethlehem. They were traveling on the fringes of their reason and intellect, barely grasping why they had embarked upon such a strange journey. But this time their reasoning was following a revelation that had arisen in their spirits, or was it their hearts? They could not explain it very well, other than they were searching for a king whose name was not Herod. They were so sure of this fact they had to courageously deflect Herod's admonitions and questions when summoned to his paranoid throne. There was blood in the air that night as a small, power-obsessed dictator tried to outwit God and foil a rescue mission that had been planned from the dawning of creation.

Christmas sums up the paradox we are faced with when we encounter Jesus. He is radical, unpredictable at times, relentless, disturbing, unafraid, and disarmingly humble in his demeanor. There is a tug of war within us; we want to make him in our image and lifestyles. "This is how I'd do it if I were God," we declare. He resists and wriggles from our hands that press him into a mold far too small for his personality and presence.

He has come to rock the status quo rather than be cradled in a manger. He is born to make all things new, set captives free, defeat the source of sin and darkness. His mission was to restore a lost humanity into the embrace of their Creator Father. We, his children, had been estranged for so long we had become conditioned to regard him as our adversary—someone to be feared rather than embraced.

December is adorned with sweet-smelling holly wreaths, gifts, shopping, lights, carols, and Christmas pageants. Nothing wrong with those traditions, if they do not lose sight of what is at the heart of the season. Advent (the four weeks before Christmas) is incomplete, only half a word; "ADVENT-URE" completes the picture. God entered a world that is broken, dark, and boringly predictable in lifestyle. Christmas highlights his ADVENT-urous Son, Jesus. "Follow me," he says, "if you dare, and live a little!"

CONSIDER:

Has your relationship with God through Jesus become too refined, small, and unimaginative, built on traditions of the past (and not all are to be discarded) but with few encounters in the present, and little anticipation for the future? What would you like to be different? Tell him.

1 CORINTHIANS 2:9

However, as it is written: "What no eye has seen, what no ear has heard, and what no human mind has conceived"—the things God has prepared for those who love him.

64 | Bold Faith

Believe for what we do not yet see.

Sometimes I get discouraged. Peter did when he looked at the waves crashing around him as he attempted to walk on water. It is initially exhilarating taking a step of faith, but sustaining that buoyancy and momentum is quite another challenge. Circumstances come crashing down, and negativity buffets like a strong wind. Faith is not about perfecting the art of denial; rather, it is looking at what seems like a Goliath and declaring who God is in the face of the threatening giant.

As a pastor, I sometimes look at our financial challenges as a church with no idea how we will break through. At one time, our church plant had been operating for three years and we were seeing little impact or growth. I noticed how we encouraged some people, while others drifted away. It saddened my heart to lose people we grew to love and care about. How can we Christians draw them in? How do we do a better job of accepting those who are different to us and introduce them to Jesus in a manner they can hear? How do we encourage others to serve rather than merely consume? These are some of the issues that raise their heads before me and, to be honest, at times they almost overwhelm.

I can be tempted to second-guess what we are doing and ask whether we have taken on too much. Did we hear God correctly? I can begin to unwittingly converse with the one (satan) who constantly feeds lies and discouragement to those willing to listen. These inner battles of thought and mind are normal—and to be expected by anyone who wants to grow in their Christian faith and see real change and transformation. We simply must learn to walk through discouragement powerfully, quickly, and deliberately.

The key to quell the lies, slay the giants, and calm the storms of unbelief and doubt is to offer a sacrifice of praise. David (the King of Israel) said that he refused to offer a sacrifice to God that did not cost him anything. This was in response to an offer from his servant Araunah to provide all that was needed for a sacrifice, with no cost or effort required from David. Praise is the easiest thing in the world to give when life is going well, money is in the bank, our job is secure, relationships are filled with joy, and our body is healthy. Frankly, it is rare for everything to align in such beautiful harmony, isn't it? The sacrifice of praise is one that I offer to God regardless of my circumstances and emotions. It is loving God for who he is no matter what. If God is good and faithful all the time, then my circumstances are not an accurate indication of whether he loves me, more or less. Nor are they a reliable expression of how he feels about me.

The worse I feel, the more I need to turn toward him; the more I need to declare the truths I know are in his word and have been experienced in my life before—demonstrations of his promises and faithfulness. I am confident that he is always good, and that he never curses me or desires me harm or suffering.

CONSIDER:

Whatever the challenges you face, choose to rise up and declare in faith:

"Lord you are faithful and have proved yourself to be sensitive to my needs in the past. I remember that you provided when I had nothing and will continue to do so. You gave me a breakthrough when I could not see the way ahead, and you will do so again. I recall how you gave me a promise that you have resources around the world and that I can trust you with finances.

"I declare before your throne that you are good and faithful, and that you are not a God of meager resources. We believe you have not established us in order that we limp along begging for support. We call on you, mighty God, faithful Father, to release resources that will enable us to do more than we could have asked for or imagined. We renounce a spirit of poverty, of doubt, and of negativity. We praise you for your faithfulness and goodness toward us. We declare your Kingdom come in our lives and anticipate release and breakthrough in the name of Jesus and to his Glory!"

Acts 4:29–31

"Now, Lord, consider their threats and enable your servants to speak your word with great boldness. Stretch out your hand to heal and perform signs and wonders through the name of your holy servant Jesus."

After they prayed, the place where they were meeting was shaken. And they were all filled with the Holy Spirit and spoke the word of God boldly.

A spoon does not know the taste of soup, nor a learned fool the taste of wisdom.

Welsh Proverb

---

65 | Declarations of Faith

What happens when you make a declaration like the one at the end of Musing 64?

Do you feel your spirit lift, in contrast to how it sinks when mired in discouragement and buffeted by big waves? Faith rises when we speak out the truth of God—a truth that is greater than and superior to what we see with our eyes, think in our thoughts, and work out with our limited logic. We are focusing on the one who has infinite wisdom, no limitations, and is aware of all things. Therefore, our hope is no longer restricted by our situation or understanding but rather is held in his infinite love. That is what a sacrifice of praise sounds like. It is a declaration of hope, precisely because we are speaking counter to the wisdom of our culture and the apparent reality of our circumstances.

It is not blind faith; it is faith with supernatural eyes and legs. Here is another source of truth about the significance of praise. In the Old Testament, the priests were commanded to keep the fire burning on the altar continuously (Leviticus 6:13). A sacrifice needs to be fueled and fed, day and night. It is a lifestyle. Fire ignites on sacrifice and will keep flaming as long as it has something to burn.

That altar is our hearts as individuals and as a fellowship. It is one of the reasons why it is so important for us to gather regularly to worship and praise. When we show up, we are adding fuel to the fire. It is why we find so many reasons to not show up regularly; satan knows that if he can distract us, the fire will not burn as brightly. We will not be as effective countering his lies and discouragement. Following Jesus increases our discernment. We become wise and get used to making sacrifices, until eventually they become lifestyle practices and the cost is more than worth it.

Finally, take note of the gates of heaven spoken of in Isaiah 60. Gates are the entryway into a city through which people and resources enter and leave. In Isaiah, the city gates are described as "Praise," set in walls called "Salvation" (verse 18). In that spectacular city of God, each of the twelve entrances has a gate consisting of a massive pearl (the pearly gates). Pearls form in oysters as a means of defense against irritants and demonstrate overcoming.

These biblical symbols and references inspire me as I trust they will encourage you. I hope it provides an explanation as to why we spend time in worship. How using our voices to declare who God is, and how we feel about him, is so vital to achieving spiritual breakthrough personally, as a church, and indeed in our city. God can transform any irritant or challenge we might encounter into pearls that become priceless in our lives and characters.

CONSIDER:

Here are more declarations to declare boldly:

Ephesians 3:20-21 Now to him who is able to do immeasurably more than all we ask or imagine, according to his power that is at work within us, to him be glory in the church and in Christ Jesus throughout all generations, for ever and ever!

Philippians 4:8 Finally, brothers and sisters, whatever is true, whatever is noble, whatever is right, whatever is pure, whatever is lovely, whatever is admirable—if anything is excellent or praiseworthy—think about such things.

Mark 11:22-24 "Have faith in God," Jesus answered. "Truly I tell you, if anyone says to this mountain, 'Go, throw yourself into the sea,' and does not doubt in their heart but believes that what they say will happen, it will be done for them. Therefore I tell you, whatever you ask for in prayer, believe that you have received it, and it will be yours."

Psalm 91:3-5 Surely he will save you from the fowler's snare and from the deadly pestilence. He will cover you with his feathers, and under his wings you will find refuge; his faithfulness will be your shield and rampart. You will not fear the terror of night, nor the arrow that flies by day . . .

66 | Peace, Despite . . .

I suppose all of us secretly dream of life as perpetual paradise: no worries or stress, zero responsibilities, the chance to relax in never-ending sunshine on a beach where the turquoise ocean rolls lazily up pristine white sand.

I remember taking a team to support a building project in Honduras. After our work we visited Roatan, one of the Bay Islands. The beaches were picture perfect, stretching for miles and lined with coconut palms, the long green fronds bending and spiked against a clear blue sky. "Why are these beautiful beaches so empty?" I inquired. "Well, if you lie near the coconut trees, you never know when a coconut may drop on your head, and the beach is full of sand fleas," was the answer given.

It seems so typical of our lives on earth, where every Eden mirage has a hidden liability or hazard, invisible from a distance. May as well learn how to embrace our present (the double-edged sword that is life) and find peace and joy where we live right now—amid falling coconuts and other bugs—because these illusory Edens are everywhere.

I am inspired by how Jesus lived on earth. His context was riddled with donkey-loads of inconvenience, unfairness, exploitation, and uncertainty. Human life was cheap; people lived at the mercy of the Roman occupying army and the whims of those who ruled. Human rights were a joke, religion was peddled on every street corner, and babies could be killed if the regional autocrat was paranoid about rumors of a newborn king.

This newborn grew into the guy who told us not to worry about tomorrow, what we will eat, drink, or wear, and promised to give us peace but not as the world gives. Jesus did not merely give advice to others—he lived what he advocated. He walked the talk without a victim mentality or a grandiose sense of martyrdom. Nowhere is that more evident than in the events leading up to his crucifixion. It was the easiest outcome in the world for him to avoid by choosing compromise or offering the religious leaders some token of respectful subservience for public consumption.

I imagine if I were in Jesus' situation, I might hear God calling me to another land as a missionary. Perhaps I could delay what seemed inevitable by advocating for the disciples to have more equipping and training. They were so raw and often teetering on the edge of packing up and returning home. My rational mind could find more reasons than the tassels on my prayer shawl to avoid sipping the cup in Gethsemane, escaping the ripping lashings, and keeping my hands out of sight rather than nailed to a cross.

Unlike me and Peter, when the rooster crowed, Jesus never flinched, doubted, or turned to run. As a faith-filled man, he wrestled through sweat and blood in the Garden of Gethsemane before his capture and crucifixion. Even his knowledge of God as Father and the power of his Spirit did not stop him from feeling fear and anxiety.

The crucial point for us is this. Long before the pressure climaxed, Jesus had settled the matter of whom he trusted when darkness loomed, when strength drained in blood on the ground beneath his nailed feet. There was peace to be experienced amid circumstances that sent every friend scurrying for cover. A more magnificent picture was being painted than anyone on earth could ever understand.

God Almighty underscored the fact that he was on a mission of love and forgiveness that would shake the foundations of the world with the resurrection of his Son. The journey between womb and tomb was perilous, hostile at times, riddled with injustice and easy escape routes. I am so proud of Jesus—grateful and indebted.

Peace is an inside job, flowing from the heart outward . . . because of God's love revealed through Jesus. If we wait until humans have cobbled together an agreement and conditions for peace, before too long we are picking up pieces. And around and around we go again.

CONSIDER:

Where are you delaying your abiding in peace? Are you waiting until a circumstance changes, perhaps when a goal is achieved, or a relationship is mended? Why not consider leaving those elements in God's hands and receiving his peace now? That does not mean those things are unimportant. They are merely inadequate as sources of lasting peace.

Philippians 4:7

And the peace of God, which transcends all understanding, will guard your hearts and your minds in Christ Jesus.

Turn your face to the sun and the shadows will fall behind you.

New Zealand Proverb

---

67 | Lessons from Nature

Many people are visual learners.

God provides all kinds of object lessons in nature that can be translated into principles for life. They are everywhere—simple nudges from him to encourage us to understand the ways of his heart and to pay attention to how things work.

We never see flowers unfurling petals in winter or blossoming in cold weather when the sky is gray with clouds and heavy with rain or snow. We know that only when the sun shines and warms the atmosphere do buds begin to swell and burst into flower.

Bulbs lie dormant in the ground, and as the seasons change, so they begin to appear as shoots in a natural response to the warming of spring. Because this annual cycle is as predictable as clockwork, we know what to look for and what to expect. We do not anticipate blossoms in winter, but we do allow for pruning. Fruit emerges after blossoms, and when they ripen, they fall to the ground. After observing how nature and seasons work, we plan and have expectations for how a garden will grow and mature in the future. We expect roses to grow on rosebushes, and if there was all bush and no rose, we would discern a problem with that plant.

Transplant this metaphor into the human dimension. We find some interesting parallels when we reflect on our life and growth with Jesus in God's Kingdom. God's love revealed through Jesus has the same impact on the human spirit as the sun has on flowers. When we are exposed to the light of his love, our hearts open and the flowers of love, joy, peace, and other beautiful qualities come alive in our characters and demeanor. Others notice and stop to "smell the roses"—the fragrance of Jesus that is around us—because we bring encouragement and hope.

Similarly, when we are distant or closed off to God's love in Jesus, we are more likely to resemble a plant or tree during winter. We become a skeleton of sorts—everything dormant with little that brings life or joy to others on the outside. And there is a distinct difference between winter dormancy, when we are still close to Jesus, as opposed to when we are far off. When we are close, he uses those dormant seasons to grow us on the inside, perhaps to strengthen and quietly refresh for what is to come. We do not feel dead or empty; it is merely a season perhaps with less frenetic activity, which is great.

A sign of maturity is being able to read the signs and respond accordingly. Too often we ignore the signs and are denied the joy of blessing or the opportunity to encourage. When we are withdrawn and discouraged, the chances are that we have lost sight of God's love. We need encouragement and help from those around us to step back into his presence so that our hearts can be nurtured, and healing can flow. Maybe there is some pruning that needs to take place in anticipation of a glorious future that will explode as soon as we experience the warmth of his love again. Similarly, when God is alive in us, it tends to show by our countenance: they will know us by our love.

What I am trying to say is that spiritual discernment, struggles, and growth are not a huge mystery or difficult to discern. The presence of the sun pulls what is inside out into the open in radiant fashion. In the same way, Jesus evokes responses in those who keep company with him. The solution to broken or discouraged human beings is not so much talk but rather helping them soak in the presence of the Son and watching what happens. There ain't no winter in heaven, and where heaven touches earth the Son/sun always shines, drawing out the good even in bad times.

Keep close to Jesus and life will flow in you and through you like streams of living water. And in times of scarcity and pruning, it does not mean that we are not loved. Pruning is the work of a caring and skillful gardener anticipating the next fruitful season. Cease pruning in a garden because it "hurts," and the neglect will translate into less fruit but an increase of foliage.

CONSIDER:

What kind of plant would you like to be? Research that plant and consider what season you may be in. Have you experienced pruning in any area over the past twelve months? How about blossoming and fruitfulness? If you were the gardener, what would you prune? Embrace the process and the season.

ECCLESIASTES 3:1–8

To everything there is a season, and a time for every purpose under heaven:

a time to be born and a time to die, a time to plant and a time to uproot,

a time to kill and a time to heal, a time to break down and a time to build,

a time to weep and a time to laugh, a time to mourn and a time to dance,

a time to cast away stones and a time to gather stones together,

a time to embrace and a time to refrain from embracing,

a time to search and a time to count as lost, a time to keep and a time to discard,

a time to tear and a time to mend, a time to be silent and a time to speak,

a time to love and a time to hate, a time for war and a time for peace.

68 | Extraordinary You

Be encouraged during the mundane and the ordinary, for discovering how to thrive in that place is the key to joy and fulfilment.

Why not read through the various Gospel accounts of Jesus' life and consider how frequently he touched lives supernaturally while he was on his way to somewhere else. He did not frantically wonder what he was meant to be doing for God (his Father); instead, he lived in a state of readiness and sensitivity to the prompting of the Spirit within. What does that look like today?

Make it a priority to spend time with Jesus every day, even fifteen minutes. I always try to do this at the beginning of the day. It sets the tone in your spirit, much like having a shower wakes up your body. Don't curse yourself with declarations of being a morning or an evening person; rather, work out how you can have coffee with Jesus. Talk to him about whatever is on your heart. Read Isaiah 37:14, where Hezekiah is in trouble. He goes into the temple with a letter bearing bad news and "spreads it out before the Lord." That is being authentic.

Jesus invited us to bring our burdens to him, and first thing in the morning is a great time to lighten up. Better to share your heart with someone who adores you, is not judgmental, and who has power to change things. Much better than to bury and deny and make mountains out of molehills. In those fifteen minutes, read a short passage from the Bible. The psalms are great, as well as paging through the Gospels, reading repeatedly the stories of Jesus and placing yourself within the encounters described. What was the person experiencing, how were they touched, what can that say to me today? What difference did Jesus make in their lives, and what is he saying to me right now? You will be amazed how he speaks with great encouragement, power, and simplicity through imagination and open hearts.

Then read through Acts about how the early church began to develop and grow. Finally, practice living from a place of favor and acceptance with God your Father. Imagine being seated at the banquet that was prepared for the prodigal son. Picture the life, the aromas, the laughter, the joy; hear the music, embrace the mood, consider the demeanor of the One who initiated the celebration. Understand that you are incredibly precious to him and that he delights in you. Resist the tendency to brush it aside in your head. Love and acceptance are the cornerstones of your new identity as God's son or daughter. Your effectiveness is him flowing through you, to release heaven on earth today!

As you step into another mundane day, affirm your identity as a beloved daughter or son, an heir to whom he has promised all his resources. Accept the fact that he is alive in you, because of what Jesus accomplished on the cross and because his Spirit lives in you—whether you feel anything now or not. Can you feel your kidneys or liver? Pay attention as you go about your day and see what happens.

CONSIDER:

You are the heart, hands, and feet of Jesus wherever you happen to be. His Kingdom is on earth alive in you, and he invites you to make it known: to pour out his grace over others who do not know what they are missing, who resist with their minds and argue with their mouths. Their empty hearts are hungry for God's love—more than they know. You could be the one to bring healing and transformation. Amid the ordinary you will become extraordinary.

PHILIPPIANS 4:8

Finally, brothers and sisters, whatever is true, whatever is noble, whatever is right, whatever is pure, whatever is lovely, whatever is admirable—if anything is excellent or praiseworthy—think about such things.

69 | Impressed by Jesus

God, birthed among his creation in human form, reminds me of the uniqueness of Christianity alongside other world religions. Nowhere else in history is there such a clear revelation of God as is found in the person of Jesus Christ—his life, miracles, death, and resurrection. His teaching and character are intertwined with his identity and his unequivocal claim to be God: "Anyone who has seen me has seen the Father" (John 14:19). It's not a statement that is inclusive, politically correct or compromising. It is a scandalous declaration—unless it is true.

Other religions brush Jesus aside or push him back in line. They relegate him with many other prophets and holy men, such as Mohammed, Buddha, Krishna, Abraham, or a multitude of other pretenders to the throne. Jesus refused to allow the opinions and agendas of those around him to define him or his mission. In fact, it was because he insisted on courageously not conforming and stepping out of line (challenging dead traditions, non-empathic leaders, and oppressive religion) that he was eventually crucified outside Jerusalem on a hill named Golgotha. He has never been politically correct or intimidated by threats. That is what impresses me and why I am proud to be one of his disciples in the twenty-first century.

I am impressed with his uncompromising commitment to truthfulness—rather than popularity or expediency—and his willingness to suffer rather than back down or waver. He defined truth as rooted in himself. Truth is a person.

I am impressed with his patience, which enabled him to wait in the wings for thirty years before his Father released him into public ministry. So many today cannot wait to be noticed and attain to the high places in their careers or ministry. Jesus patiently trusted his Father with the timing. His entire life was about submission, service, and following his

Father's agenda and heartbeat. Later he would pass those values on to his disciples, encouraging them to learn to abide in his Father's love, much as branches are grafted into grapevines.

I am impressed by Jesus' easy interaction with people from all walks of life, without exhibiting favoritism or prejudice. He was a friend to the broken, the lonely, the intellects, leaders, and those who clung to the frayed edges of society as outcasts. His compassion was unlimited; he was always willing to be interrupted by the ones whom most others walked past without sparing a glance or a thought.

I am impressed by Jesus' bold and risky faith, which led him to walk on water, summon Lazarus from death to life, and believe in Simon Peter long before he understood the calling on his life. If anyone was naturally supernatural, it was Jesus. He refused to posture or perform miracles to impress or to enhance his reputation. Every miraculous event was a response to an obvious need, whether the person was crippled, bound, or infirm and needed to be set free.

I am impressed by the love and loyalty Jesus displayed to his disciples, whom he called his friends. He entrusted his mother into the care of one of them. He responded to the genuine doubts and struggles of Thomas after the resurrection. He went out of his way to draw alongside a despondent and broken Peter when he failed to live up to his own boasting. He welcomed disreputable women like Mary Magdalene into his entourage where she found a new identity, deliverance, and healing. He washed their feet as he faced death and the brutal trauma of crucifixion. He loved unconditionally.

I am impressed and humbled to the point of tears that Jesus reaches out to me and never gives up on me; that he has time (more than once or twice) to drape his arm across my shoulders and encourage me with love and acceptance.

I am so impressed and grateful. All I can do is say thank you as I ask him to make me more like he is, on earth as in heaven. May my heart be transformed so that his love imbues all my thoughts, words, and actions.

CONSIDER:

What impresses you about Jesus? What can you thank him for?

PSALM 103:1–5

Praise the Lord, my soul; all my inmost being, praise his holy name. Praise the Lord, my soul, and forget not all his benefits—who forgives all your sins and heals all your diseases, who redeems your life from the pit and crowns you with love and compassion, who satisfies your desires with good things so that your youth is renewed like the eagle's.

There is no shame in not knowing; the shame lies in not finding out.

RUSSIAN PROVERB

70 | Orphan Mentality

Most of us appreciate receiving encouragement to grow in confidence as disciples of Jesus; of learning about his huge resources that we have at our disposal. When I spoke of this at a gathering recently, at least a third of those present asked Jesus to release them from an orphan spirit—into their true identities as sons and daughters. Sound strange? Think of it like this. If God merely wanted a bunch of people who kept rules and were obedient, he could have left us with the Old Testament and sent angels to whip us into shape. We would be his servants, and he would be our master lauding it over us from a distance that would cause us to revere and fear him.

Ask people whether they believe in God, and the reply will often be, "I believe in a God; there has to be something behind this world . . . but I don't really give the matter much thought." Perhaps God is not quite so distant. He reveals himself in his Son Jesus, who died on the cross for our sins so that when we die, we can go to heaven. That's another common Christian paradigm among churchgoers. The mindset is one of appeasing God and surviving on earth until we die; then, at last, we will experience release and happiness.

Again, the reality check application leaves us surviving on earth and making the best of it, with God at least in the background. He is the one to whom we appeal when all else fails. We are tempted to blame him for disasters and suffering. In these times, our posture before him is one of, "What have I done wrong now?" The orphan spirit is cultivated in such understandings and environments. Hallmarks include a sense of inferiority, poor self-esteem, insecurity, confusion, little trust, and a poverty mindset. The orphan has little or no sense of belonging, of being loved as a son or daughter, or of being welcomed and accepted for who they are.

Orphans constantly strive for acceptance and significance through performance. They tend to passively resign themselves to fate. "If God wants xyz, he will . . . " They seldom ask for anything, either because they do not feel worthy, or they are afraid of being rejected and disappointed, or even because they feel too proud to do so. Consequently, when it comes to God, there are no expectations and zero passion. The mindset may come through rejection and negative experiences, and once embedded it is tough to shake off.

The bizarre thing is that when we thumb through the stories of Jesus' life on earth, we discover that he is constantly reaching out to the lost, the lonely, the sick, the downcast, and those who are oppressed by life. He models love, friendship, interdependence with his Father, and a power to heal that is astounding. He literally tears up the rule book and offers relationship through forgiveness and a divinely initiated invitation to feast with him at a banquet.

Jesus restores identities and draws all whom he calls into a tight-knit group of friends for mutual support and a sense of adventure. Living life on earth as sons and daughters of a loving Father with resources to empower, release, and bless is quite different indeed. The prodigal son received the revelation of his Father's love when he least deserved it. The older brother remained on the outside as an orphan (while his brother rebelled away from home), when for years he could have enjoyed all that he had access to through his father. After his brother returned, his father reached out to restore him with equal passion and affection. Sometimes the hardest hearts can be found in those closest to home who appear faithful and obedient on the outside. In other words, they conform outwardly but inwardly rebel and have attitude. There are so many layers in all of us that God's Spirit of truth wants to shine his light on.

CONSIDER:

Do you feel like a beloved son or daughter, or do you more easily relate to the orphan? All orphans can transition into much-loved sons and daughters, usually by being shown the way through friendships. Jesus said, "Love one another. As I have loved you . . . " (John 13:34). We cannot give away what we have not received.

LUKE 15:31
"My son," the father said, "you are always with me, and everything I have is yours."

71 | God is Faithful

Someone reading this—perhaps even you—needs encouragement to know that God is faithful; that he can be trusted if you remain close and refuse to allow your circumstances to have the last word. "Then why doesn't he do something for me?" you might retort with weariness and tired unbelief. That is certainly what I would have said some years back when I was neck-deep in despair and angrily trying to work out life "doing it my way." Trying to push my will onto the world around me and unwilling to consider that I needed help.

It was an exhausted me who finally began to yield and admit once again that I cannot do life on my own with any sense of fulfilment or satisfaction. My best efforts left me empty inside, and my worst moments filled me with anger and blame. That is when I heard the whisper reminding me of my true identity: "You've forgotten who you are. You're my beloved son, with identity and value. There's a future waiting for you if you'll step into it . . . all I have is yours." I felt power rising on the inside of me, and in my mind's eye my circumstances receded as I grew in assurance and stature and, in Nelson Mandela's words, began the long walk into freedom.

Nothing magically fell into place the next day. It was more like beginning a long hike through valleys and over mountains. The unknown journey was one step at a time across varied terrains. Sometimes it was beating through the thick underbrush of a dark valley; on other days there were inspiring views from the summits of mountains. As I walked, I noticed my faith muscles growing again. I was becoming more easily able to endure the uphill climbs and even enjoy challenges that would previously have led me back into despair. The secret was that I knew I was not walking alone; my trust in God my Father's presence and provision blossomed and was constantly reaffirmed. In my spirit there was a new sense of hope and confidence. I had a renewed sense of self and an expectation for a better future that had been a long time coming.

There were dark nights of terror and doubt, but joy invariably came in the morning; often music and songs were on my lips. The music had been silent for a long time. I was learning to live and walk from a place of victory, provision, and assurance. Above all, a renewed identity rooted in God's love and favor rested upon me all the time no matter what my circumstances were.

Today I feel like a veteran, a seasoned fighter, one who is supremely confident in the faithfulness, integrity, and purposes of Jesus. I want to serve him, and through him enable others to experience his reality and know the same affirmation he has poured over me, despite my rebellion at times.

CONSIDER:

Do you have challenges that are stifling your faith? Is disillusionment or discouragement thwarting your efforts? These are moments in which we will benefit from sharing our thoughts with someone we can trust. Sometimes merely bringing things into the light helps to turn them around and stop the rot.

Here is a reflection from my friend Kyle who helped edit these writings:

Today, I ask you to imagine God, the creator of all things, the one who never makes mistakes, entering his creative studio. The door swings open, and light fills the space. God, with purpose in his eyes, quickly grabs an ancient leather apron, tosses it on, and starts pacing back and forth—inspiration has taken hold of him. Soon he begins to inspect thousands of clay mounds on a shelf near the back of his studio. He is looking for something particular, something well suited to his intentions. Suddenly he finds the proper bit of clay and smiles a smile that only mothers have for their newborn babies and lets out a resounding "Yes!" You watch as he sits down gently, and skillfully he moves the clay from one place to another until the rough shape of a human being is formed. Then you hear him begin to hum to himself, as with his fingers and tools he brings forth the fine details. You begin to recognize this clay; to your surprise and unbelief it looks like . . . like . . . you! He begins to admire his work. It is beautiful in his eyes; tears of joy fall upon his face. He cannot wait to share you with the world, and so he takes one enormous inhale until his chest hurts and breathes his spirit into you and says, "Live my child, live!"

2 Timothy 2:13

... *if we are faithless, he remains faithful, for he cannot disown himself.*

*God gives the nuts,
but he doesn't crack them.*

German Proverb

72 | Running the Race

"Spectacular achievements are always preceded by unspectacular preparation."

—Roger Staubach, American professional footballer

When we think of the Olympics, we picture athletes competing on a world stage for the honor of winning a medal and celebrating a unique accomplishment. When the winner stands atop the podium, we hear the backstory as to how they arrived at such a glorious pinnacle of achievement. Some may thank God for their gift and talent; others may not.

You can be absolutely sure that we'll never hear this: "I prayed every morning for God to make me into a top athlete and then I went about my day. One morning I woke up and my muscles were strong, and I was capable of performing at a level I'd never imagined—with no training, no time invested, no role models, no effort at all on my part."

No one will stand on a winner's podium who has not spent years practicing, learning, and pressing through pain barriers to realize their dream. Not a single athlete will have made it alone without the help of a team, a trainer, supporters, and the confidence of those who believed in them. I am not stating anything other than the obvious.

We laugh at the suggestion that an athlete could win a race by praying and not training. Many who profess to follow Jesus are quite indignant when told that such a strategy does not work when applied to daily life either. We isolate ourselves, have no role models, shun training, consult with no coach, and seldom if ever show up for practice— and then wonder why we never make any progress. We point fingers at God and others and question why we are not winning more races. We struggle in life, breathless and unfit, and declare that God does not care or never seems real to us . . . and nothing changes. Silly, isn't it?

If someone randomly clambered down from the bleachers and could participate just because they "felt like trying"—and won—we would never believe it to be true. We know what it takes to be an Olympic athlete. Here's the thing. Athletes not only build muscle and skill on the outside; they also develop strong characters, the ability to persevere, and learn how to keep going when the race gets tough.

The Christian life is a journey that requires coaches, friends, feedback, training, character building, and maturing.

CONSIDER:

Consider the investment athletes make and dare to ask God to speak to you about your training program in his arena. There are things ahead of you that he would love to release in you—things that will take your breath away and thrill you with amazement. Don't settle for the mundane and mediocre; get involved and see what is possible. Where can you perhaps increase your "training"? Are you humble and willing to learn from others and ask for help? Are you familiar with your strengths and weaknesses?

Hebrews 12:1–3

And let us run with perseverance the race marked out for us, fixing our eyes on Jesus, the pioneer and perfecter of faith. For the joy set before him he endured the cross, scorning its shame, and sat down at the right hand of the throne of God. Consider him who endured such opposition from sinners, so that you will not grow weary and lose heart.

73 | Risky Living

My two friends Jimmy and Dave were sitting outside, their motorbikes gleaming in the bright sunlight. We chatted for a while and then I went up to Jimmy's bike, kicked the tire, and said, "Can I take it for a ride?" Looking a little apprehensive, he turned the key, and the bike roared into life. I climbed on and tentatively set off around the corner—it had been twenty years since I had last opened the throttle of a big bike. I rolled into the parking lot and accelerated. The power and thrust forward was exhilarating. Ever since I have been saying, "Must get a bike again!" The sense of freedom and adventure it offers is an aspect of life that often seems to disappear with age, busyness, and perhaps discouragement.

God speaks in strange and fun ways at times. I have been reviewing a book series called "Wild at Heart" by John Eldridge. It is designed particularly for men, calling them to step into the adventure God always intended for men to live in the company of Jesus. Of course, God desires the same for women, but it seems that some men tend to relegate "faith and Christianity" to something less than masculine and equate it to boring church attendance. In the book, five guys/friends spend eight days at a ranch in Colorado and share together a journey of self-discovery involving much physical activity and personal reflection. Their ultimate focus is to reach into their hearts and find a life and passion that for most has been hidden and lost for years. Discovering a vibrant faith means refusing to settle for the status quo and allowing God to draw us deeper into the life he yearns to release to us, and through us. We cannot feel the blood rushing and our hearts pounding by watching TV, or sitting in an armchair, where the only gain is an increased risk of a heart-attack from a sedentary lifestyle. Too many people play it safe and are bored to tears by their lives. Instead of stepping into the adventure, they blame others for their predicament and wallow in self-pity or anger at life's unfairness and God's indifference. I know, I was there—for too long.

That is why Jesus never asked people to watch him. Instead, he called them to follow him without any explanation of where they would be traveling together. He did say that if we are to find life, we must be prepared to lose it first, by which he means to let go of our controlling and small-minded approach to our lives. Wouldn't it be a shame to live our entire life within the confines of a matchbox only to discover Jesus invited us into a magnificent mansion containing too many rooms to count? Blame, passivity, fear, and hopelessness is the currency of those living far from God and Jesus.

Let us help one another draw close to him and encourage the boldness to emerge. No one can live life for another; do not wait for change—step into making a difference as God works in you first. Or as a friend reminded me, "Nobody can do your push-ups for you." It may be responding to or initiating what seem insignificant tasks or relationships right in front of you. I do not know if I'll get a motorbike, but I am committed to "being alive" as a servant and disciple of Jesus, fueled with passion for an adventure that may from time to time even be risky. How about you . . . want to keep yawning or hold on tight and invite Jesus to go for it!?

CONSIDER:

Do you want your life to have greater meaning and depth? What would be exciting for you in your next step with Jesus? Perhaps it terrifies you at the same time. Talk to him about that and ask for an opening, a nudge, an opportunity. See what happens.

HEBREWS 11:7–8

By faith Noah, when warned about things not yet seen, in holy fear built an ark to save his family. By his faith he condemned the world and became heir of the righteousness that is in keeping with faith.

By faith Abraham, when called to go to a place he would later receive as his inheritance, obeyed and went, even though he did not know where he was going.

74 | Freedom and Contentment

One of my great joys and privileges has been working with an addiction recovery group called "I am Second." It has opened my eyes to how difficult it is to overcome substance abuse.

Discussion around the problem of alcoholism, street drugs, and prescription medication invariably leads us to consider the impact on daily behavior as the dependency takes hold. Withdrawal elicits a heightened craving and a demand for gratification no matter what the cost. Some of us succumb, and others manage to avoid that particular pathway and can be quite disdainful in our attitude toward "addicts."

However, the human capacity for gratification is not limited to the obvious and humiliating behaviors of a random beggar on the street, or a girl shooting heroine in a back alley. The love of money and materialism is probably a greater addiction worldwide than any other human shortcoming. It is respectable and commonplace (often promoted as healthy) to the degree that we measure self-worth, success, and importance by dollars, cars, houses, and cruises. We proudly mouth words of wisdom about working hard and reaping the rewards. In fact, this is only true in some instances—where there is a stable environment and an economy base to sustain consistent access to daily work for daily bread.

Millions of people work incredibly hard merely to scrape by and have shelter and food. Where am I going with this? I am challenging myself with the reminder of how privileged I am. I ask myself whether I really appreciate enough what I already have, and how God sees me amid all my stuff. Do we ask God for more, or are we willing to hear him ask us to "do with less"?

Numbers, Chapter 11, describes the people of Israel wandering in the desert on their journey from slavery into freedom. At first, they cried out to the Lord for freedom from Egypt. We know the story of Moses challenging Pharaoh, the subsequent plagues, and the Lord eventually winning them their freedom. They marched out of Egypt with gold and silver, no longer slaves but free, with the promise of a great future as they followed Moses and the Lord toward the Promised Land. They were protected from Pharaoh's armies, crossed the Red Sea, and were given manna to eat during their journey.

In this chapter, the people start complaining that they are sick and tired of manna, and in their discontent, we read: "The rabble with them began to crave other food and again the Israelites started wailing and said, 'If only we had meat to eat! We remember the fish we ate in Egypt at no cost—also the cucumbers, melons, leeks, onions, and garlic. But now we have lost our appetite; we never see anything but manna!'" (Numbers 11:4–6).

The Lord's response is one of measured anger at their ingratitude. He provides them with meat in the form of quail. When challenged by Moses asking "how?" he answers, "Is the Lord's arm too short? Now you will see whether or not what I say will come true for you" (11:23). This exchange between Israel and the Lord makes me think of my attitude and sense of appreciation and gratitude for what he provides.

In their greed the people of Israel fantasized about free fish in Egypt when they themselves were slaves. I do not need more things for me to be free or content. I am free. My prayer is that we will be joyful, thankful, and recklessly generous, just as God has been with us.

CONSIDER:

What would it be like to receive everything you need from Jesus and the Holy Spirit right now? Peace, love, joy, contentment . . . rooted in them not in circumstances? No need to wait!

ACTS 18:9–10

One night the Lord spoke to Paul in a vision: "Do not be afraid; keep on speaking, do not be silent. For I am with you, and no one is going to attack and harm you, because I have many people in this city."

75 | The Real Battle

Judas (backed by Roman guards and Temple leaders) betrayed Jesus with a kiss in the Garden of Gethsemane; Peter drew his sword, ready to protect Jesus. Like many of us, he missed the point when he sliced through the ear of one he perceived to be his enemy. His focus was understandably locked on his immediate physical surroundings. But Jesus came to open our eyes to another realm.

Jesus battled the unseen realm of evil that energizes men and women to choose violence and anger over compassion and kindness. It is so hard to believe there is more to life than the merely tangible—what we can see with the naked eye. Consider the "invisible" germs and infection that the invention of penicillin effectively defeated. How about the ozone layer? I remember sitting in the sun after we landed in the Cook Islands en route to New Zealand. We were warned that the sun burns fierce there because of the depleted ozone layer. I was used to sunshine from Africa, but sure enough, within twenty minutes I could see my skin burning from the effects.

The battle around the cross was merely the tip of the iceberg in terms of all the activity taking place. While Peter was wielding his sword at human flesh, God the Father was working out justice for human sin and rebellion through Jesus facing the cross. The Father and Jesus were not really fighting satan or evil in a contest between two equals. They were treading satan underfoot with authority and power—providing the antidote for those infected by his demonic schemes and pathetic egotistical plans. While Peter had no idea of the scale of the battle he was involved in, fortunately for all of us, Jesus did.

Jesus rebuked Peter and made a stunning comment. He told him that he did not require his sword to defend him. "Do you think I cannot call on my Father, and he will at once put at my disposal more than twelve legions of angels? But how then would the Scriptures be fulfilled that say it must happen in this way?" (Matthew 26:53-54).

The week leading into Good Friday is one of violence and turmoil, courage amid fear, cowardice, bullying, brutality, religion gone mad, love refusing to cower or back down. It is probably the most remarkable week human beings have ever witnessed—or ignored. A week when God showed the full extent of his love and willingness to enter suffering for the sake of you and me. "My God, why have you forsaken me?" Jesus screamed as he hung in agony on the cross. He bore upon himself the full weight of sin, shame, and guilt—the toxic waste of human rebellion.

Jesus went to the cross to take the punishment we deserve, in order that we can go to the cross and receive the reward he deserved. There is a tactic that is instantly recognizable whenever satan is at work. Fear separates us from one another and causes dissension. Today we don't have floggings and whips; we have suppressed anger, polite exchanges, and individuality that isolates and weakens the whole. It was blatantly obvious around Jesus as he approached the crucifixion. Jesus emphasized to his disciples the absolute priority of their relationships being guarded and cemented with love. Love draws people together and attracts the presence of God. With God's presence comes power to overcome, and victory.

CONSIDER:

Let us ask God for eyes to see behind the scenes, so we avoid drawing figurative swords to slay the wrong enemy. Ask God for confidence to always know his presence, and wisdom to let him fight the real battle. What do I attend to and what do I leave well alone?

JOHN 15:12-13

"My command is this: Love each other as I have loved you. Greater love has no one than this: to lay down one's life for one's friends."

76 | Community Has Power

He is risen!

The realm of satan and evil detests true community. Where relationships draw people together, the power of love in Jesus is substantially increased; mutual protection is dynamically enhanced, and the manifest Kingdom of God forces darkness to flee. In other words, light blazes forth—power for healing and overcoming surges.

In our culture of individual preferences and lack of tolerance for inconvenience or personal sacrifice, the church is too often reduced to dead religion, providing entertainment or spiritual self-help to keep everyone happy. Of course, there should be fun, music, education, and many messages of love and personal fulfilment. But the message of Easter is about God breaking the stranglehold of evil so that we can live free as servants and warriors of his Kingdom! It's not about bringing sandwiches to the sick; it's about power to heal and transform.

Jesus' resurrection and quick return to the disciples demonstrated how much he valued them. He understood their failure to follow through on some of their promises. He refused to take offense. Instead, he took the initiative to restore their relationships and lavish forgiveness and new beginnings upon his friends. What a demonstration of evil being conquered! In the same manner, God is calling us to mature and to demonstrate such mercy and forgiveness among ourselves.

The church is ravaged by those licking their wounds and holding offenses that cause ongoing destruction, isolation, and ineffectiveness in a world awfully familiar with such a lifestyle. If Jesus is risen and lives within us, then we have a mandate to be salt and light, impacting our environment for good rather than being slaves to attitudes and circumstances that cause us to draw swords way too readily.

Let us learn to value our relationships and guard our hearts against dismissing others or withdrawing. We require discernment to know whom God is drawing us alongside and when to step back (boundaries and limitations). Just as the events leading up to the cross caused the followers of Jesus to scatter, so the reverse happened after the resurrection. As Jesus appeared in his astounding resurrection victory, his disciples received a Spirit of courage and unity that was the foundation of the Christian church. Community and friendship around the resurrection is a powerful proclamation of the Kingdom!

CONSIDER:

Are there any relationships or situations around you where an initiative from you could build a bridge or possibly facilitate restoration? Are you harboring offense? Perhaps you may consider asking forgiveness? Be a relationship builder and restorer in the name of Jesus.

Ephesians 4:1–3; 25–27

As a prisoner for the Lord, then, I urge you to live a life worthy of the calling you have received. Be completely humble and gentle; be patient, bearing with one another in love. Make every effort to keep the unity of the Spirit through the bond of peace . . . Therefore each of you must put off falsehood and speak truthfully to your neighbor, for we are all members of one body. "In your anger do not sin": Do not let the sun go down while you are still angry, and do not give the devil a foothold.

77 | Expectations of Church?

I WAS REMINDED OF a conversation with a schoolmaster in England years ago when he proudly stated, "I regard myself much like a flying buttress; I support the church from the outside." I am sure we would all agree that church is so much more than buildings and history. But what does that "so much more" look like?

Peter describes the church as a human building of living stones being formed into a community by God himself through Jesus and the Holy Spirit. He spoke from experience, as he found himself—one crude pebble—picked up on the shores of Galilee by Jesus, the master craftsman.

He was known as Simon in those days, a fisherman who probably never imagined his life ever reaching beyond the hills surrounding Galilee, or his hands doing more than casting nets and cleaning fish. He was a roughly hewn stone, poorly educated, and certainly not within remote consideration of being appointed as a leader in the church of his day. That church was a Jewish synagogue with clear guidelines and rules administered by an elite clergy/rabbinical hierarchy. Who would have thought that when God walked this earth in the person of Jesus, he would eventually scout for his leaders on beaches and in marketplaces?

Jesus was familiar with the inside of synagogues and the temple, having spent many years of his childhood and early adult life undoubtedly enduring some challenging services and teachings. It seems that breaking the mindset of the establishment and building a band of revolutionary disciples could not be accomplished at the same time even by the Son of God. Almost everyone I talk to has experienced disillusionment with church and expresses opinions about what is lacking, wrong, or frustrating. Some opt out and live on the fringes, strongly asserting that they can follow Jesus without bothering with church.

Let us imagine walking alongside Jesus on the shores of Galilee, comforted by his preference for being outside the walls of the institution. Yet Jesus regularly attended synagogue and adhered to the Jewish feasts and festivals in Jerusalem. Although he grappled with the religious leaders of his day, he did not undermine or seek to destroy the community of believers inevitably and always forming around the love of God. This is underscored when we bump into Peter, who used to be Simon.

"What happened to you?" we gasp, as we see before us a stone transformed into an exquisitely shaped rock exuding confidence and strength without the slightest hint or smell of fish.

"Jesus picked me up in my boat—surrounded by fish and nets—and began to chisel away at my character, worldview, identity, self-confidence . . . everything actually."

"How did he do that?"

"He invited me to follow him wherever he happened to go, and I said yes. There was something about him that captivated me. But more importantly, he looked at me and spoke into my life. He imparted to me a belief that there was far more in the future than I ever considered possible . . . He believed in me!"

"That must have been wonderful."

"It was . . . and the most stretching and challenging time of my life at the same time."

"How so?"

"When he took hold of me on that beach, he gathered a bunch of other rough stones to travel with him as well. I became testy until he pointed out to me that whenever I would cast the net into the waters of Galilee my intent was to catch more than one fish at a time. He said that he wanted to build a new community where many would voluntarily swim into his nets because they would be so desperate for rescue and change. He taught and demonstrated a lifestyle and language I had never heard before—about God's Kingdom on earth, power to heal, and loving one another even to the point of death. He called God 'Father,' and in his presence I witnessed a life that was rich and full."

"What changed for you?"

"For the first time, I experienced a community around Jesus where learning and formation took place as we traveled together day and night, in good times and terrifying moments. We shared our experiences and, on many occasions, had to bear with each other in our inappropriate responses and attitudes. I certainly messed up. But every time, Jesus insisted on gathering us together to work out the challenges. In the end it was only Judas who decided to bail and take another course. That was painful because I loved him like a brother and had hoped he'd resolve his differences."

"What do you want to say to the church today?"

"If you have a personal relationship with Jesus, then trust him with the journey he has you on . . . and don't give up on the process. Do not disregard your relationships; believe him for your future, particularly when you cannot see the way ahead, in the company of those he has brought you together with. You are living stones; there is more chiseling and shaping to come, but it is worth it. Keep your heart wide open and be teachable!"

CONSIDER:

If you were God holding you in his hand, what would be the next area of your life and character to chisel, mould, refine, encourage, and shape? Who in your life right now might God be using in that process? And where could he be using you in the life of another? Decide to be a co-laborer rather than a resister.

1 CORINTHIANS 3:7–9

So neither the one who plants nor the one who waters is anything, but only God, who makes things grow. The one who plants and the one who waters have one purpose, and they will each be rewarded according to their own labor. For we are co-workers in God's service; you are God's field, God's building.

78 | Closer Than We Realize

I WAS IN A hurry as I ran out to the car. "Darn, I forgot my glasses!" I went back inside and looked in the normal places but could not find them. Scratching my brow in a subliminal attempt to activate the aging brain, my fingers brushed against an object perched on my head. "Oh my, they've been there all the time . . . glad there's no one around to see this," I muttered and smiled as I raced back outside.

Most of us probably have similar stories in which what we are looking for is either on us, in our pocket, or right before our eyes. When we finally clue in, we are stunned at how blind or absentminded we can be at times. What about God and his Kingdom? If we read slowly through the pages of the Gospels, we might be amazed and encouraged to learn that the people around Jesus failed to discern who he was. How could they?

He was so different from what they expected. He looked like them, talked with their accent, dressed in their clothes, and superficially at least appeared to be just another teacher with a new spin on God. Some of that changed when he reached out to heal the sick and multiply loaves and fish before their very eyes. On one occasion, Jesus was surrounded with leaders and Pharisees asking, "When will the Kingdom of God come?" Jesus replied that the Kingdom is not tangible or objectively visible: " . . . the Kingdom of God is in your midst" (Luke 17:21). All that the people saw before them was a man. In fact, the Kingdom of God was closer to them than they ever would have dreamed possible! They failed to comprehend the possibility of the supernatural and extraordinary being resident within the mundane and ordinary.

On another occasion, two men were walking on the road to Emmaus lamenting the crucifixion of Jesus and the death of their hopes. A stranger drew up alongside in sandals and they engaged in a lengthy discussion. They shared their forlorn thoughts with him. He opened the Scriptures and gave another perspective that caused their hearts to burn within them. It was only when they invited him for supper and he broke bread at their table that the scales fell from their eyes. They saw the Kingdom—the risen Jesus in their home! Then he was gone.

One of the biggest blind spots we can have is a closed mind. Limited vision and preconceived ideas place so many limitations on God that he has nowhere to move within the confines of our lives. We can drown him out with our ideas (limited), experiences (lack of), fears (usually unfounded), cynicism (negativity), until all we are left with is religion and doctrines devoid of passion or power. On the other hand, if we recognize how easily we slip into those earth-bound places—how we become blind to the awesome love, presence, and burning life of the Kingdom in Jesus—then we can do something about it.

God is not disillusioned with us. We can ask God's Spirit to open our eyes and ears to the presence of his Kingdom "in our midst." Watch all heaven break loose. Life does not have to be the same again. Neither need we look back and wish with longing and a sense of having "missed the bus." Step forward in hope and expectancy for the more that is still to come . . . believing is seeing! God is on our side in our quest to know him. He's not making things more difficult; he's a best friend and your friend—always.

CONSIDER:

Ask God to reveal to you something precious that has been right in front of you and that you have overlooked. He often speaks extraordinary truths through the ordinary around us.

MATTHEW 6:25-27

"Therefore I tell you, do not worry about your life, what you will eat or drink; or about your body, what you will wear. Is not life more than food, and the body more than clothes? Look at the birds of the air; they do not sow or reap or store away in barns, and yet your heavenly Father feeds them. Are you not much more valuable than they? Can any one of you by worrying add a single hour to your life?"

79 | Death

I have death on the brain right now—death and dying. Cheerful thought, isn't it?

Yes, it is. I am not thinking of death and dying in terms of a terminal illness but rather as a caterpillar might contemplate disappearing into a cocoon. Does a caterpillar know what lies ahead with any degree of certainty? Doubtful. Does it have any anticipation of emerging one day as a butterfly, of entering an entirely new identity, utterly unrecognizable and able to soar beyond the bush that's been its home since infancy? Perhaps this resonates with you, too. Imagine if the only way into the Kingdom of God is through a cocoon. No caterpillars in heaven, only butterflies with faint recollections of being confined to crawling up branches and eating leaves.

Heaven begins on earth, with outspread wings and the sweet nectar of flowers, drifting high in the breeze light as a feather. If we think of ourselves as caterpillars for a moment, then the "death" of our caterpillar selves would not be so bad knowing that it is merely a gateway to another, more glorious self. Seems to me that many are hoping and praying to pursue relationship with Jesus and be citizens of his Kingdom on earth while maintaining a caterpillar persona. It ain't gonna happen.

Caterpillars believe in God and love Jesus. They worship him in holy huddles on branches across the universe. In fact, First Caterpillar Chapel Choir is world renowned for their harmony, melody, and musical expertise. They gaze wistfully toward heaven and dream of the day they will fly in the sweet by and by. Right now, they would rather not die. Instead, they sing songs, dream of heaven, never get to fly, or heal, or live with extraordinary power. They have lost sight of the vision—that being a caterpillar is a pathway to becoming a butterfly, not an end.

I share deep empathy with the caterpillar angst and mentality regarding transformation and change, particularly when I am not sure what life in a cocoon will feel like; will it even work? Most cocoons we experience will be formed out of relationships and circumstances that may seem like death for a while.

Jesus promises that anyone who is prepared to lose their life (go into the cocoon or "die" like a seed) will come alive! Sounds like resurrection—or butterflies unfurling. Jesus used the metaphor of a seed falling into the ground and "dying." It disappears. As it abides in the ground it bursts into a life that would be impossible if the seed insisted on lying dormant.

You might think to yourself, *If God wanted me to be anything else he'd have made me different.* Maybe embracing the mystery and unknown is an essential part of life with God. Many of the gifts within us are not immediately visible. Clues to their existence may lie in our dreams, in what piques our interest. Then, it is up to us to take baby steps to give them wings. God will meet you more than halfway in the most unexpected ways.

CONSIDER:

Do not be too quick to discount what may be possible for you. Remember Peter? He had no idea what God would do with his life when Jesus called him to follow. It was more of a challenge for him to walk on land than perhaps to walk on water.

JOHN 3:3–7

Jesus replied, "Very truly I tell you, no one can see the kingdom of God unless they are born again."

"How can someone be born when they are old?" Nicodemus asked. "Surely they cannot enter a second time into their mother's womb to be born!"

Jesus answered, "Very truly I tell you, no one can enter the kingdom of God unless they are born of water and the Spirit. Flesh gives birth to flesh, but the Spirit gives birth to spirit. You should not be surprised at my saying, 'You must be born again.'"

80 | Fathers

"A truly rich man is one whose children run into his arms when his hands are empty."

—Author Unknown

It would have been impossible for Jesus to be God on earth in human form without a deep and intensely affectionate relationship between him and his Father. God the Father spoke audibly over his Son twice during his earthly life. The first time was when he was baptized by John: "You are my Son, whom I love; with you I am well pleased" (Luke 3:22). One can hear the pride and affirmation in the Father's voice as he publicly encourages his Son on the threshold of launching into his life's mission. The second is when Jesus is on the mountain with a few friends, and they have a supernatural encounter with Moses and Elijah. "This is my Son, whom I love; with him I am well pleased. Listen to him!" the Father says to Peter, James, and John (Matthew 17:5).

During his three years of public ministry, Jesus was unashamed to express his dependence upon his Father or acknowledge the fact that he could accomplish nothing without him. His entire life rested in the hands of his Father. Imagine jumping into a dark chasm where you cannot see the bottom and all you hear is, "Trust me, I'll catch you." When Jesus was born as a baby in Bethlehem, every day of his earthly existence was entrusted to his Father in heaven. The only day their relationship was broken was as Jesus hung upon the cross, separated from his Father (because of our sin). For the first time in his life he shouted, "My God, my God, why have you forsaken me?" (Matthew 27:46).

It should come as no surprise that the father is incredibly significant in the formation of every human being's identity as a son or daughter, man or woman, father or mother. We are created to be secure in a father's love and to be affirmed and supported by a father's touch and words throughout our lives. Some of us unfortunately have been living lives with a "father-shaped vacuum" inside us—the result of absentee dads, abuse, neglect, or estrangement. The good news is that Jesus came to heal that void and promised that after his resurrection no one need ever be an orphan or fatherless again.

A key to finding freedom and wholeness in our earthly lives is to make peace with whatever our experience has been with our earthly fathers. If you grew up in a home with a loving and supportive father, then give thanks to God. Present or absent, they have a significant impact upon our self-worth, identity, gender, sexuality, and more. Burying anger, hurt, or disappointment never heals or releases freedom. Finding validation, acceptance, forgiveness, and understanding (usually with at least one person walking alongside us in whom we trust) is a constructive path forward. Many I have counseled have struggled with God as "father" because of their experience with their human fathers. God is much kinder, nicer, gentler, and more truthful than anyone we will ever meet on earth. He grieves when we grieve. He permits (because of free will) what he often does not delight in or approve of.

CONSIDER:

How is, or was, your relationship with your father? How does it impact your relationship with God as your Father? One way to gain a better perspective is to explore what God is like, with him as Father as the focus. Look at Jesus to know the character of the Father. More than anything in the world, he wants to reveal himself to you.

MATTHEW 11:27

"All things have been committed to me by my Father. No one knows the Son except the Father, and no one knows the Father except the Son and those to whom the Son chooses to reveal him."

81 | MONEY

"The value of a man resides in what he gives and not in what he is capable of receiving."
—ALBERT EINSTEIN

HEALTHY CHRISTIAN COMMUNITY PLACES high value on honesty, transparency, and open communication. For most of us that is a challenge because we are perhaps more accustomed to hiding, avoiding conflict, or taking the road of least resistance. You know what I mean . . . peace at any price; not wanting to hurt feelings; assuming things rather than checking in. Not everyone is safe, and we do not want to be hurt.

Let's talk about money.

Money has significant spiritual power. The quickest way to discern how strong it is in our lives is to consider how generous we are—how easily we part with it. Most people do not have enough money—in their estimation—and would love to give more, "if I could afford it . . . " Ironically, that tends to be the response from people who are quite rich in the context of the world's economy. The most generous church I have ever seen was in Africa among people who did not have much but who shared what they had with great willingness and sacrifice. I suspect the poor in communities have a greater sensitivity to their mutual needs and interdependence; it is key to their survival.

I am invariably reminded of the time when a group of us, all students, met for a Bible study in a friend's apartment in Cape Town. We had known each other for most of our teenage years, attending youth groups and growing up together. Sheila had recently returned from a year studying in England. She had met the man who would later be her husband and wanted to complete further courses but was short of the funds to make it happen. We agreed to pray together and ask the Lord to supply her need.

As we prayed, I remember looking around the group and counting how many were present. The thought popped into my head that if we were each to contribute a relatively small amount of dollars Sheila's needs would be met by us! I interrupted our prayers to exclaim, "We have the answer right here—we are the Lord's gift to Sheila!" It was so exciting to see the revelation spread and everyone clamber on board. We asked God to provide, and he opened our eyes with a solution that ultimately was not a great sacrifice, but it blessed Sheila profoundly.

When we discuss tithing, we're referring to 10 percent merely as a basic benchmark. I am aware that some churches have used the tithe in rather legalistic (this is what the Bible teaches) ways. The whole topic of finances is too often presented as legalistic and oppressive, with guilt as the main motivator. Giving is meant to be in response to our gratitude to God for the love and grace he has lavished on us through Jesus.

The tithe is more of a starting point. If we had time to go through the teaching, we'd discover that giving only begins over and above a tithe. After all, looking at it another way, we could conclude that we get to keep 90 percent, thus reducing our giving to a legalism that is far too restrictive. That is like couples who nitpick about how they share their resources; if the focus is "how much you give, how much I give" the relationship is doomed. When the emphasis is on the relationship, then the sharing is even more extravagant and never an issue, because it flows from a place of love, appreciation, honor, and respect. Remember how Jesus responded to the widow whom he observed placing a few pennies into the basket as her offering of thanks to God? He blessed her, because in percentages she had given so much more than others with far greater wealth and resources. We could also talk about tithing time and talents as another expression of gratitude.

CONSIDER:

This reflection may well raise more questions, which I encourage you to ask and discuss with someone you know and trust. There is no stupid question. How do you exercise and express generosity to others? It could be time, finances, listening, or serving in some capacity. There are many ways to give above and beyond money. And then, how easily do you receive? Do you allow others the blessing of helping you in the same multitudes of expressions of love and kindness?

LUKE 6:38

"Give, and it will be given to you. A good measure, pressed down, shaken together and running over, will be poured into your lap. For with the measure you use, it will be measured to you."

Pride is concerned with who is right; humility is concerned with what is right.

PAKISTANI PROVERB

82 | Pursuing

An imaginary conversation among a group of acquaintances, perhaps in a coffee shop. Snow lies on the ground outside and fog mists the windows. They could be men and women, young or old, you and me.

"Fishing and hunting are what I love," says the man with laughing eyes. With thick fingers he clutches a silver spoon and stirs his steaming coffee.

"What's the attraction?"

"It's an adrenalin rush—time in the most beautiful cathedral in the world. That's where I find God, you know . . . nothing else like it."

"But you have to spend a fair amount of money on equipment, often travel significant distances, get up early in the morning, experience discomfort and perhaps danger, and sometimes even come home with nothing?"

"That is true. When one hunts or fishes it's not only about the kill or the catch, but also everything involved that makes the whole experience worthwhile, especially with a bunch of friends. Of course, hooking the 40-pounder or bagging the moose is the ultimate. Have I ever told you the story of the big guy with massive antlers I nearly brought home? It was just north of One Hundred Mile House, and we'd been—"

"I detest hunting or fishing," someone mutters across the table. "In fact, anything 'outdoorsy,' as they say, leaves me cold, literally and figuratively."

"That's ok; let's talk about quilting or baking, reading, skiing, sailing, swimming, studying, sports, traveling, building, gardening, exercising, and anything else we can think of."

"What's your point?" the indoor cynic asks with a suspicious sigh.

"If I had to choose, it would be reading biographies. I do enjoy the stories behind the lives of people."

"There's no trick question; I'm merely making the point that passion is what keeps us alive and gives meaning to what we do from day to day, don't you think?"

"Suppose so."

"When I mention God, do you get the same rush of passion?" I lean across the table toward the hunter and the reader, and the question pops out and collapses like a huge elephant between us.

"Hell no," says the hunter, gazing out the window. "Tell you the truth, makes me uncomfortable. Reminds me of my grandmother telling me to wash my hands and sit quietly at the table. I'm not the religious type. If there is a God, as I said, I find him in the mountains."

"I'm not sure," the reader whispers. "Too many people around me, makes me uncomfortable and I don't understand why this world isn't a better place if God loves it so much. I leave the topic well alone—same as politics; it causes too much tension between people . . . "

Sound familiar?

Jesus said, "Seek first his kingdom and his righteousness, and all these things will be given to you as well" (Matthew 6:33). He could have used other words that might convey the same thing: "Look for God like you'd launch your boat and set the line for a big fish, or how you'd break a trail to hunt a moose, or when you bury yourself in a good book." We have often heard the phrase that once you've tried something, you'll be hooked. God understands that we are people of passion, and that is precisely where he wants to reveal himself to us. Jesus encouraged people to ask, knock, and look. And we will find.

The degree to which we pursue something is the degree to which we delight in it. We will no more get excited about Jesus by sitting around waiting than we will catch a fish by cleaning the tackle every day in our living room.

CONSIDER:

By now you should have a sense of where your passion is with Jesus, in comparison to other areas and interests in your life. If your light has grown dim, know that he is right beside you as you read these words, his hand on your shoulder. "What do you want?" he says. "Let's go and get it; don't be afraid."

JOHN 10:10

The thief comes only to steal and kill and destroy; I have come that they may have life, and have it to the full.

Better to be slapped with the truth than kissed by a lie.

RUSSIAN PROVERB

83 | Caring for Others

"Why bother with addicts and people who are difficult to love and demonstrate little desire to change? People have choices to make, and if they don't want to take responsibility let us rather support those who do."

Those are sentiments and responses many of us consider as we reflect on the life-debilitating needs and challenges people face around our community. What is helpful? What is enabling? When are we getting in the way, and when are we merely washing our hands of a responsibility we prefer not to face? Honestly, I'm pondering these questions most days. About the only response I am sure of is that we can't do nothing and claim to be disciples of Jesus.

Perhaps looking at Jesus' actions, insights, and teachings will be illuminating. When I consider walking away from a difficult person and abandoning them because of their stubborn attitude, their lack of appreciation, and/or their destructive choices, I have one simple question: "What if this were my brother or sister, son or daughter?" Jesus always asks me that question. Sometimes the answer is to leave them be for a while. I cannot walk away completely—not while they are still breathing, particularly when the person behind the addiction or struggle has a name and I have glimpsed their delightful and often humorous personality traits beneath the grime and distortion.

Consider Jesus' story of the Good Samaritan crouching at the side of the road to tend to the wounds of a broken man—with no agenda other than he had eyes to see and the resources to give in a situation others chose to ignore. On another occasion, Jesus was having dinner with a respectable Pharisee, Simon, and a disreputable woman wept over Jesus' feet and anointed him with oil. Simon was indignant at the messiness and emotion of such an encounter around his table. Jesus was appreciative and totally understood where the woman was coming from. With disarming simplicity and tenderness, Jesus said to Simon, "You gave me nothing when I entered your house, in contrast to this woman's outrageous demonstration of affection."

Simon, it seems, had little awareness of his impoverished spiritual state. He clung for his identity and sense of worth to the title and status of Pharisee and religious leader. The woman, on the other hand, had no buffer or ability to hide; she knew only too well the depths to which she had fallen and how out of control her life had spiraled. It seemed that "spiritual people" she encountered judged her and avoided her—that is, until she met Jesus. It was his compassion and outstretched heart and hand that transformed her life to a degree that no words could express. Gratitude welled up inside toward one who, for the first time in her life, offered forgiveness, acceptance, and hope for a future. Her words spluttered awkwardly out amid sobs and tears. As she was anointing Jesus' feet, she suddenly realized she was making a mess and had nothing to clean up with. She used her hair as a rag, such was her unrehearsed confusion and fumbling thanksgiving.

CONSIDER:

Do you find it easy to empathize with the suffering of another? Can you love the sinner and hate the sin—in your own life as well as in the lives of those around you? Meditate on the fact that Jesus loves you every day the same, no matter what you have or have not done.

LUKE 10:30–37

In reply Jesus said: "A man was going down from Jerusalem to Jericho, when he was attacked by robbers. They stripped him of his clothes, beat him and went away, leaving him half dead. A priest happened to be going down the same road, and when he saw the man, he passed by on the other side. So too, a Levite, when he came to the place and saw him, passed by on the other side. But a Samaritan, as he traveled, came where the man was; and when he saw him, he took pity on him. He went to him and bandaged his wounds, pouring on oil and wine. Then he put the man on his own donkey, brought him to an inn and took care of him. The next day he took out two denarii and gave them to the innkeeper. 'Look after him,' he said, 'and when I return, I will reimburse you for any extra expense you may have.'

"Which of these three do you think was a neighbor to the man who fell into the hands of robbers?"

The expert in the law replied, "The one who had mercy on him."

Jesus told him, "Go and do likewise."

*You may go where you want,
but you cannot escape yourself.*

NORWEGIAN PROVERB

84 | Loving the Difficult People

I USED TO BE a lot more like the man who walked by, on the other side of the road, in the story of the Good Samaritan . . . until I was the one lying bleeding and found myself isolated, in shame, with rocks thrown by those maintaining their distance. Jesus found me somewhere out there and loved me back to life despite "me." As I read the stories Jesus told and the encounters he had, I invariably find myself on both sides of the proverbial fence, or road. "I once was lost, but now I'm found, amazing grace how sweet the sound . . . "

Where does that leave me answering the question about why we bother with frustrating, rebellious, and unappreciative people who make the wrong choices? There is some selfishness in my answer. I notice that when I dismiss people with addictions or ongoing struggles, keep a distance, and have too many self-righteous opinions, it is not long before I am sharing a sumptuous meal with Simon—except on these occasions Jesus is absent. The conversation has a negative edge, and my demeanor is noticeably lacking in compassion or empathy. I justify myself with articulate speeches pulled from my intellect attached to eloquent theories, much like windchimes or the sound of clanging gongs. At least they drown out the cries for help from the street. My mind is active but my heart grows cold, and Jesus withdraws. Our relationship falls quietly to the wayside; I cease growing in maturity and fail to view the other as a brother or sister.

In contrast, I'm aware that when I open my heart and step across the road, knock on doors, and call hurting people from their hiding caves, my heart is pounding crazily—even though my mind is bewildered. Jesus is right there, and an irrational hope and faith rises to believe that the Spirit of God will pour out healing and life even through my fumbling attempts. *If that were my daughter, I'd never give up trying*, I remind myself. *Remember where you once were when Jesus gently blew dying embers into rising flames within you.*

A servant heart and an irrational love for the lost and desperate are no-brainers once I have been carried home on the shoulders of the shepherd who left ninety-nine others just to find me. In fact, my greatest privilege is hearing him send me out to do the same. How often? As many times as is needed, for as long as it takes, until everyone is found and restored to the family. "Greater love has no one than this: to lay down one's life for one's friends" (John 15:13). This was the mandate for the church in the first place. To be a community where hurting people will be loved and accepted as they are introduced to Jesus and encouraged in their journey with him.

Everyone has a name given by Jesus that calls forth the destiny and hope he has placed within us to be released. Most are conditioned to be identified by a problem: "Hello, my name is John, I'm an alcoholic and have been clean for three days." What if Jesus wants to encourage us to know a better future and to be identified by where we are going instead of what we have been? Simon grew into Peter, Saul into Paul, and you and I are becoming more than we could ever have imagined.

CONSIDER:

Do not give up on anyone. Naturally, we have lots to learn, and there are inevitably rough spots along the way. Be inspired by Paul who eventually was so confident of his new identity in Jesus that he wrote the words below.

PHILIPPIANS 1:3–6

I thank my God every time I remember you. In all my prayers for all of you, I always pray with joy because of your partnership in the gospel from the first day until now, being confident of this, that he who began a good work in you will carry it on to completion until the day of Christ Jesus.

85 | Peace

"What good is it for someone to gain the whole world, yet forfeit their soul?"

—Mark 8:36

Mark records the words of Jesus spoken into a culture not unlike ours, in which people looked for peace in all the wrong places. Jesus promised his disciples a peace beyond understanding and assured them that God, his Father, was quite aware of their needs and would provide for them. He encouraged them to learn from the birds and flowers and see how he nurtures them and will do the same for his people. We may hear his words, but then, seeing flowers cut and bundled into a vase, and a bird becoming roadkill, we splutter, "Yes, but . . . "

When reflecting on peace and worry, it helps to read the letter to the Philippians. Paul writes as a Roman prisoner or, as he prefers to be known, an ambassador in chains. In the first chapter, he acknowledges that some are preaching about Jesus with mixed motives and questionable agendas. Having stated the situation, he shrugs it off and says, "But what does it matter? The important thing is that in every way, whether from false motives or true, Christ is preached. And because of this I rejoice" (1:18). Later he tells us that he has learned to be content in all circumstances, "through him who gives me strength" (4:13).

The disciples approached Jesus with the news that someone was driving out demons in his name. They tried to stop him because he was "not one of us." Jesus was infuriatingly unthreatened and unperturbed, responding, "Do not stop him . . . for whoever is not against you is for you" (Luke 9:50). On other occasions, the disciples wanted to prevent children from bothering Jesus, and he told them to let them come to him. A blind man shouted out for his attention, and the disciples fussily told him to keep quiet. Again, Jesus disregarded them and ordered them to bring the man to him. When Jesus visited the house of his friends Mary and Martha, the sisters got themselves into a disagreement because Mary sat listening to Jesus instead of helping Martha. Martha was indignant and pleaded with Jesus to have Mary help her. Jesus was totally uncooperative, exhorting Martha to cease her well-intentioned bustling and chill out with her "lazy" sister.

When Jesus was sailing with the disciples on Galilee, he took the opportunity to catch up on sleep. In the meantime, a storm blew up, and the disciples lost it with fear and anxiety. They shook Jesus awake, screaming above the wind and the crashing waves, "Don't you care that we're terrified?" As fishermen, they knew they were in real danger. Jesus certainly did not weep with sorrow and beg their forgiveness. Instead, he challenged them for their lack of faith and proceeded to calm the storm. Left to himself he probably would have carried on sleeping and let the storm play out.

When Jesus was preparing the disciples for the time when he was no longer with them, he promised them the Holy Spirit. He would be a Comforter, an Advocate, who would teach them as they lived life. He assured them that the Holy Spirit would be to them what his Father was to him. In his absence they would not have to live lost as orphans in the world.

CONSIDER:

Do you struggle with anxiety, worry, or lack of peace? It is common for many. It helps to thank Jesus for his love and presence, and affirm that he has our lives and circumstances in his hands.

JOHN 14:17–18

But you know him, for he lives with you and will be in you. I will not leave you as orphans; I will come to you . . .

86 | Overcoming Anxiety

JESUS PROMISED THE DISCIPLES a gift of peace that was completely different from the peace the world had to offer. He told them, "Do not let your hearts be troubled and do not be afraid" (John 1:27). In contemporary language, "Don't worry!" On the evening the disciples were locked behind closed doors after the crucifixion—scared out of their minds—he suddenly appeared in his resurrection and said, "Peace be with you" (John 20:21).

Peace is a big deal to Jesus. I think it is because he wants those who follow him to experience peace—not as the world gives, not as tranquillizers enable, not as monetary security purchases, not as things we do and acquire in the pursuit of peace. It's a quality of peace that builds from the inside. Peace is the by-product of knowing the love of God the Father firsthand. We cannot find peace by chasing after it. We receive peace in the company of Jesus as his Holy Spirit comforts us on the inside. Orphans feel lost and worried; sons and daughters of the King of Kings know they are provided for and are confident in the provision and resources available to them from heaven. Our challenge is to dare to test God's faithfulness and kindness. Instead of rolling your eyes as you read this and saying, "I wish," how about giving God permission to lead you deeper into the truth of these words?

This is not theory. I used to be one of the most nervous and insecure children you could imagine. I was afraid of everything and worried about every aspect of my life for years and years. Gradually, as I walked with Jesus, the anxiety left; I don't know how or when exactly, it just did. Then, when I decided to abandon our relationship and "go it alone," I rediscovered anger, anxiety, stress, and the weight of self-reliance. I looked for fulfilment on my terms and discovered depression and antidepressants, followed by years of struggle at every level of my life. Finally, as with the prodigal son, I came to my senses and my reconciliation with Jesus and the Father restored a peace that was beyond my understanding. There were anxious moments along the way, but when God came through and proved his faithfulness it made peace a little easier to experience.

I am still growing and learning to trust and am encouraged that anxiety is not a frequent visitor anymore. How about you? Maybe this week Jesus merely wants to quietly embrace you and whisper "Peace be with you" in your ear. Allow him to teach you to walk in peace, which is invariably a by-product of staying close to him. If you try to understand the process merely intellectually, it can be elusive. Relationship with the Prince of Peace may be the key.

Peace recognizes that the weight of the world and even my circumstances does not rest upon my shoulders alone. God is fully invested in me and my welfare. It is comforting to know that he has my life and welfare in his hands and that I can trust him at every twist and turn of the journey. If I make a mistake or wrong choice, he will continue to love me and to help me reboot and recalibrate to get back on track.

CONSIDER:

There is nothing shameful about acknowledging anxiety, so be free to talk to him about that. If you invite Jesus to love you and you give him access to your heart, peace will not be far behind. Joy and hope will squeeze in there too—from the inside out. It is all paid for by Jesus and rooted in him. Our responsibility is merely to receive. The Lord bless you, keep you, make his face shine upon you, and give you his peace.

JOHN 14:27

Peace I leave with you; my peace I give you. I do not give to you as the world gives. Do not let your hearts be troubled and do not be afraid.

87 | INTO THE UNKNOWN

SOMETIMES I LOOK AT the computer screen and wonder what words will come from my fingers to fill the page and be helpful or encouraging. There are days when my heart beats with passion and I have a word to communicate that excites me, and then other days—like today—when I have no clue. What does one do then? I decided to experiment and merely begin to write and tell you what my starting point is: to trust God and see what happens. It feels like Peter stepping out of the boat or I guess beginning to stride into a Promised Land that looks at first glance much the same as the ground covered yesterday. Except, as one begins to move and step out in faith, the Red Sea parts, the blind man sees, the weak become strong, the weary are lifted up, the downhearted receive hope, and emptiness is filled with everlasting joy.

How does it work? I do not know the answer in exact terms. I do know that as I am writing now the message is dawning, filling the sky with all the colors of a sunrise, where once it was blank and empty. The Spirit of God is like the wind and sometimes the faintest of whispers. I was driving home with a friend the other day and we were talking about hearing God's voice. He told me how he had a mentor that kept pressing him for more when he was giving words of knowledge. He challenged him to press in beyond the obvious, to take some risks, to see what happened even if he was not right every time. But the advice that lodged in my memory was, "Listen for the faintest whisper and go with that one—it's probably God." Why does he work like that? I do not know. I am saying that a lot.

I guess it is because following Jesus in the Spirit is a fragile and beautiful journey that demands traveling sight unseen, much as I am following my fingers across this keyboard right now. On one hand I feel as if I am just filling the page; on the other, this is a simple exercise in trust demonstrating how faith works.

If you feel stuck, begin walking in any direction and tell God your Father that you're trusting him. If you can't sense his love, start thanking him that he loves you and for his hand holding yours right now. He likes you and knows precisely what you need. Remember, he's the adult in the relationship and will communicate with you in a manner that you can understand and hear. Relax and believe; he'll speak loud enough, even with a whisper. Trust your heavenly Father to catch you, and for God's sake, jump!!!! "But I feel nothing!" you protest. That doesn't matter; your feelings are not the bedrock of your faith—Jesus' faithfulness is. He wants you to rest in the "knowing" even as you have no idea what that means. He told me years ago to do that. How? Pay attention to what is at hand and do whatever is in front of you. If the grass needs mowing, mow the grass . . . and allow the future to unfold.

Over the past years one of the major character growths he's been forming in me has been a combination of faith and patience—to believe for what I can't yet see or have control over. This is where what began with confusion and blankness crystalizes into revelation and truth and becomes the whole point of this page. It's about taking risks and having an adventure with God who loves, plays, and never ever abandons us. He desires us to know his faithfulness while at the same time growing during everyday life. He wants us to experience in real time, today, how willing and able he is to back us up and release good fruit when we could only see "nothing."

He focuses on process and character, not so much on goals and arrival points. And here we are, another page written. I do not know about you, but I'm inspired! Trust him.

CONSIDER:

Are you waiting around for the perfect time, the full picture, the voice telling you to get going? Chances are it will be a long wait. Step out and do something—write, paint, talk, initiate, and then follow the thread. Do not be afraid of getting it wrong; perfection is not the point. Start anticipating learning, course adjustments, and surprises . . . and have some fun along the way. God does not paint by numbers, and neither should we.

Matthew 17:20

Jesus replied, "Because you have so little faith. Truly I tell you, if you have faith as small as a mustard seed, you can say to this mountain, 'Move from here to there,' and it will move. Nothing will be impossible for you."

---

*God conceals himself
from the mind of man,
but reveals himself to his heart.*

Aᴀfrican Pʀoverb

---

88 | Finishing Well

It is a long flight from London to Vancouver. Whenever I can, I make sure I have an aisle seat to enable me to walk around and stretch without disturbing others. About four hours into a flight, I wandered to the back of the aircraft and looked out of the window over a vast expanse of snow and ice stretching as far as I could see. The sun lit up undulating white landscapes overlooking an ocean of cracked ice where nothing on the surface gave any hint of life or presence. *This wouldn't be a good place for an emergency landing*, I mused. Fortunately, the pilot stayed on task, the engines kept working, and five hours later we landed in Vancouver—in the rain.

I really appreciate the fact that airlines have a great reputation for flying passengers to a chosen destination, usually completing their flight on schedule. Such reliability is what the business is founded upon and enables those utilizing the service to plan events around their practice of consistent delivery. "Finish what you start," parents tell their children. We probably all remember the excuses that bounced from our lips like popcorn: "I'm tired . . . I'll do it later . . . I don't feel like it . . . Something else came up . . . It wasn't what I expected . . . " and so on. There is always a moment when we hit the proverbial wall. We can either press on without the initial passion we once had for the project, or we can stop altogether and bear the consequences.

Our tendency is to not complete, not stay the course, be distracted, bail out, and generally lose momentum. It is one of the primary reasons we get stuck in our relationship with God—or lack thereof. It is because we don't understand that following Jesus is not the same as flying an airplane from point A to point B. God is not goal oriented or fixated on moving us from one place to another as quickly and efficiently as possible. Rather, his aim is to develop character in us that transforms who we are. He accomplishes this while we journey with him day by day in the company of others. He is entirely committed to finishing what he began, so when we wander off, he waits for us to return to his side. He can transform any negative and build it into a positive for our development and learning. Everything can be redeemed, and nothing is wasted.

Embarking on journeys in airplanes is about changing our external environment; journeying with Jesus is about transforming who we are from the inside out. Completing what we start has nothing much to do with getting the best marks or gathering incredible amounts of information. It is more to do with being reliable, developing a servant heart, and putting other things aside when the consequence of my choice is more challenging than I anticipated. It involves building integrity and trusting God to work in us through the sometimes-tedious process of merely showing up. This means believing God when we feel nothing, because that "believing" is called faith, and that faith gives God something to work with.

Perhaps it is about surrendering control of our agendas and trusting God with our hearts, lives, and growth.

CONSIDER:

The Holy Spirit tends to focus us on two things in life: how to trust the Lord and how to be trustworthy ourselves. We are in this together, so let us encourage one another along the way. How are you doing in these two areas? Here is an invitation to keep growing and learning.

Paul talks about his passion for completing the race of his life strong and well.

PHILIPPIANS 3:12

Not that I have already obtained all this, or have already been made perfect, but I press on to take hold of that for which Christ Jesus took hold of me.

PROVERBS 3:5–6

Trust in the Lord with all your heart and lean not on your own understanding; in all your ways submit to him, and he will make your paths straight.

89 | Step Out

The heart of God the Father is to encourage and equip us to step into the adventure of living with him that we were always designed for; to not settle for the safe and status quo but rather to dare to reach for more. In the prevailing worldview, the tired and rather bland focus for life and priorities tends to focus on surviving, vacationing, satisfying, retiring, having, playing, and reluctantly dying. God's focus is entirely different. He demonstrated through Jesus that life is to be experienced most fully in knowing his love on the inside—through serving, healing, helping, sacrificing, giving, receiving, inspiring—so that your joy may be full!

Remember when the fishermen Simon (later named Peter) and the brothers James and John were first called by Jesus? He invited them to follow him and leave the safety and familiarity of their boats and nets; to embark on a journey into the future with him that they would never have imagined possible. It all rested on their willingness to risk, let go, walk, and trust. What inspired them to do such a crazy thing in the first place?

I am sure it was because they met Jesus and witnessed his power firsthand as they cast their nets in broad daylight and caught boatloads of fish. He captivated their hearts and imaginations by his demeanor, his teaching, his authority, and his power. After Jesus' death and resurrection, he appeared to them again on the same shore and called them out of their disillusionment, despondency, and sense of failure and shame. They had been shattered by his crucifixion. They had run away and hidden, placing their safety first when he needed their company and support during his worst hours.

Jesus called those same men back to his side and reassured them of his love and mission. He once again invited them to follow him. Even in their weakness they were empowered with his Spirit. All one must do is read Acts (the account of the early church) to see how changed and transformed they were. I imagine if they had merely looked after their own interests, continued fishing, bought new boats and better nets, formed a fishing franchise, and played it selfish and safe, we would not know about Jesus. We only know of the love of the Father and the extraordinary good news of Jesus today because people of every generation undoubtedly took similar steps of faith and gave away their lives in the service of God and others. Now it is our turn.

Jesus is always on the move. God has a destiny and purpose for each of us to walk into if we would like to. It is the pathway to us becoming more alive, invigorated, inspiring to others, and finding the longings of our hearts fulfilled. However, the risk involves letting go of the ordinary. There will also be trouble, opposition, misunderstanding, and sometimes unjust suffering. We only come to terms with the strength of the grip the world has on us when Jesus looks us in the eye and says, "Follow me." Usually, he does that in the context of community and relationships, speaking through people we know. But it can also be something we read, a dream, a quiet sense, or an idea. God can speak in countless creative ways.

CONSIDER:

Pray that we will be hungry, humble, open, teachable, and willing to grow. God is calling us to step out, reach out, and believe that he has an amazing adventure ahead of us—if we will drop our nets and follow. It might not be as dramatic a change as it was for the fishermen; some will be encouraged to keep their nets and boats and follow Jesus right where they are.

MATTHEW 4:18–20

As Jesus was walking beside the Sea of Galilee, he saw two brothers, Simon called Peter and his brother Andrew. They were casting a net into the lake, for they were fishermen. "Come, follow me," Jesus said, "and I will send you out to fish for people." At once they left their nets and followed him.

90 | Discovering Treasure

Treasure hunts are never passive; they always encourage a sense of excitement, promise, motivation, and action. When Jesus invites us to follow him, it is as though we've been asked to join him on the ultimate treasure hunt, and as we walk with him, we experience similar feelings of eager anticipation at what awaits us in our journey with him. In another sense, when we are first "found" by Jesus, we get a taste of what it is like to be rejoiced over and treasured ourselves; we are his treasure. For me it came as a wave of relief and joy as acceptance and belonging washed over me. There was hope and expectancy as I anticipated a future that was not merely dependent on my ability and grit. God promised to be with me and even to go ahead of me. Best of all, his promise was to never leave me nor forsake me. How does that sound as you read this?

How do you think of yourself before God the Father? The truth revealed by Jesus was that when he takes our hand and looks at us, he sees a treasure of infinite value and worth. Remember how the father ran out and embraced the prodigal son as he returned from life on the pig farm (see Luke 15)? This was after he had squandered his inheritance on wine, women, and who knows what else. He returned to his father feeling anything but treasure-like. He felt shameful, awkward, embarrassed, and guilty. The treasure had been ripped out of him because of his rebellion, actions, and attitudes. We are often ruthless with ourselves when we contemplate our failures and regrets. Shame is a terrible friend. Shame accuses and destroys the soul. God never shames. He convicts us of wrong, calls us to repentance (change direction), and reminds us of our identity as beloved sons and daughters.

The good news is that God the Father and his Son are brilliant at restoring what looks like junk into the treasure that it was first created to be. They can do it with astounding speed—up close and personal—only when they are embracing the one who has lost hope, identity, and vision. All this talk of treasure highlights a truth that most of us need to keep rediscovering and allowing God to "make alive again" within us. That is the passion and excitement to expect new things and astounding revelations as we keep company with Jesus. We must build on the foundational cornerstone that we are loved.

In the last book of the Bible, Revelation, Jesus speaks about restoring the church in Ephesus to its "first love." To restore our first love and excitement is only evidenced when we are close to him and aware of his love and of ourselves being treasured. Jesus said that we are to love (or treasure) others as we ourselves have been loved.

If we are to walk into the promises and dreams the Lord has for us, it is critically important that we walk into those dreams from a place of confidence, love, and security in our identities as followers of Jesus and children of a loving Father. This is not sentimentality; it is the key to authority, sharing mercy and grace, and hearing the voice of God. It is the key to knowing his presence and worshiping him with an enthusiasm that is life-giving and power-releasing.

CONSIDER:

Let us ask God to release in us a sense of anticipation and expectancy—as if we were on a treasure hunt. Let us expect him to have placed a treasure amid our present triumphs or failures for us to discover and enjoy. These nuggets may come in the form of a dream, a picture, a song, a healing, or something else. Expectantly give him permission to use us. It is even possible that his treasure for someone else will be wrapped up in us! Be a participant in discovering the answers we seek. Happy treasure hunting!

1 PETER 2:9–10

But you are a chosen people, a royal priesthood, a holy nation, God's special possession, that you may declare the praises of him who called you out of darkness into his wonderful light. Once you were not a people, but now you are the people of God; once you had not received mercy, but now you have received mercy.

91 | SUNSHINE

JESUS SPENT MUCH OF his time in the region of Galilee, where the sun shines long and hot upon water reflecting the azure blue of a clear, cloudless sky. The lake is surrounded by hills of wildflowers, scattered villages, and yellow wisps of grass that bend in the afternoon breeze. Of course, holidays were not in the vocabulary of most people who lived in the times of Jesus, although the Romans and wealthy did lounge around nearby Tiberias.

The warmth and brightness of the sun brings a lightness to our mood and evokes an openness in our spirit that is almost irrepressible, much like a flower in bud, when exposed to the warmth, must blossom. With all those great qualities, there is one thing we cannot do in the presence of the sun—look directly at it. The radiantly glowing burning mass of fire is too bright and will blind us if we attempt to hold its gaze. The next best thing is to enjoy the moon in the night sky, which reflects something of the glory and brightness of the sun while having no source of light of its own.

All these images speak to me of the God we are seeking to know who has revealed himself in Jesus. Jesus evoked the same kind of response in us as the sun does during the summer months. He came to earth, was crucified, and rose from the dead to specifically invite us to discover the truth about the generous and loving God in whose mind and heart summer days were conceived and created for his children to enjoy. That is the image and reality of God in whom we are invited to experience joy, hope, and great expectancy. That is the kind of God whom our friends and neighbors thirst and hunger for without even realizing their longing.

We cannot see or look directly at God. But we can explore and discover his presence and character revealed in the historic figure of Jesus who walked the summer shores of Galilee over two thousand years ago. You and I can be like the moon to others, revealing something of God's light and glory in the way we love, speak, and unconditionally care for them. We have plenty of opportunities to invite Jesus to use us to bring some hope and comfort into someone else's night sky; to point them to the reality of an incredible God and Father whom we are just beginning to get to know ourselves. It may be through a simple gesture, a word of encouragement, a book, a cup of coffee. It does not really matter what it is.

CONSIDER:

How might you intentionally share the love of Jesus? Be mindful of those around you and creative with the expression of love. Ask for opportunities, and enjoy the adventure of being his hands, feet, and heart to one who probably is unaware of what they are missing.

MATTHEW 5:14–16

"You are the light of the world. A town built on a hill cannot be hidden. Neither do people light a lamp and put it under a bowl. Instead they put it on its stand, and it gives light to everyone in the house. In the same way, let your light shine before others, that they may see your good deeds and glorify your Father in heaven."

92 | Meals

Four meals I had, in four different countries, stand out as occasions when thankfulness was the table upon which the food was set and gratitude the plate from which I ate.

While at college in England, I was given an assignment to spend a week leading a mission in a church where a team would be hosted and live in the community for the duration of our visit. Invariably we were invited out for meals in local homes. That week in Lancashire in the North of England was no exception. One evening I was seated at a table with a family about to dig into a delicious meal of chops and vegetables. Before saying grace, our hostess explained, "I have to tell you that this meal is a gift from the Lord. When we volunteered to have you over for a meal, we trusted that the Lord would provide. Yesterday we had nothing to serve on your plates. Times have been hard and there is little to go round, and no extra. Last night the local butcher called and said someone had canceled an order and he had a package of chops for us—of course, I rushed right over."

I remember the woman's face beaming with humility—a radiant testimony to the faithfulness of Jesus who cares about every hair on our head and every chop on the plate. Twenty-eight years later, that simple act of faith—inviting guests before there is a meal to serve—lives on in my heart and encourages my spirit to keep trusting.

Almost ten years prior to that, I was in the last few weeks of military training in South Africa and had spent a day sightseeing in the region where our camp was situated. A man named Michael—one of the men with whom I had trained—invited us to his home not too far away on the outskirts of a neighbouring town. The army is not a very refined place, and quite frequently at mealtimes an officer would comment that there should be no complaints about food as some of us were being supplied with more than we would get at home. I dismissed the statement as nonsense, until we drove to Michael's home. He had grown noticeably quieter as we approached the crest of the hill before the little shack came into view. As a young man without much experience of the world, I was shocked to see a "white person" live in such squalor. We entered the little house through a backdoor that led from an outside fireplace into a small sitting area. Rickety chairs and a few upholstered chairs with stains and stuffing exposed were all the furniture in the place. Dinner was a teaspoon of mash potato (smaller than the lump in my throat) and a modest piece of meat on a cold plate. To say it was humbling is an understatement.

Another time I ate meals for a week with young orphan boys in Uganda. We were seated on long benches arranged in a square in the courtyard of the shabby concrete compound in the slums of Mbarara. When it rained, we tucked ourselves against the walls under the eaves as we devoured piles of cassava, beans, and perhaps a little meat. The decor was awful but the spirit of the boys, their laughter, and their gratitude for a safe place to live and regular meals was evident. Their joy was contagious and drew me closer to them as they blessed me with their generous welcome. Thankfully, a new dining area inside has since been created, and the bubbling chatter is undiminished.

My most memorable meal was a dry piece of flatbread, an apple, and an orange placed on a large rock in the shade of a small tree. I had spent the morning wandering in the hills of Galilee absorbing the atmosphere of the region where Jesus fed the multitudes. Peter and John had trawled the waters rippling under a blue sky, and the disciples would have walked these hills behind Tabgha (the shoreline where Jesus may have called those men to follow him). On a hot day in July, I stood alone by the rock and broke the bread as I looked toward Capernaum shimmering in the distance. I thanked God from the bottom of my heart for the gift of his Son—the Bread of Life.

CONSIDER:

When in your life so far have you felt closest to God? Do you have a memorable meal or a recollection of when you have seen him in another person? Has he supplied a need that seemed miraculous? Remember and give thanks. Perhaps it is time to host a simple meal with friends, or even those you do not know too well. Jesus loved meals with people from every background. They can be a venue for friendships to grow, vulnerability and intimacy, and very importantly, fun and laughter.

Matthew 26:26–28

While they were eating, Jesus took bread, and when he had given thanks, he broke it and gave it to his disciples, saying, "Take and eat; this is my body."

Then he took a cup, and when he had given thanks, he gave it to them, saying, "Drink from it, all of you. This is my blood of the covenant, which is poured out for many for the forgiveness of sins."

An ox remains an ox, even if driven to Vienna.

Hungarian Proverb

93 | Our Father

THE LITTLE GIRL STOOD at the end of the bridge clasping the tiniest of swords in her right hand, a look of apprehension on her face. On the other side of the bridge a mighty army gathered, pouring out of the forest, a formidable and frightening force far stronger than anything she could ever overcome. The commanding officer raised his sword in defiance and kicked his horse into a gallop across the bridge toward her. It was then that Aslan roared, and the mighty lion by the young girl's side unleashed a power that caused the river to rise and overwhelm the approaching enemy. It's one of the final scenes from the Narnia series, *Prince Caspian*, by C.S. Lewis.

It is a story highlighting the reality of good and evil. How the lust for power corrupts and distorts. How doing the right thing and walking by faith demands patience, courage, and resilience, sometimes in the face of overwhelmingly frightening and negative circumstances. In the background all the time is the quiet and confident presence of Aslan the lion—God. Many profound truths are most clearly articulated within the simple lines and pictures of a children's story. Truths about love and forgiveness, friendship and courage, hope and purpose—good overcoming evil.

What is the children's story version of a loving Father? Someone who loves me unconditionally and believes in me. Someone who is always pleased to see me and embraces me with joy, whose knee is the most secure throne upon which I could ever be seated. Someone whose eyes affirm me and who provides a place of safety, warmth, and comfort. Of course, he will discipline, rebuke at times, and perhaps evoke responses of rebellion and anger in me as I push back and test his resolve. But at the end of the day, I am secure in his love and I cherish his wisdom. Knowing that he is around is a source of great strength and peace, particularly if I can share with him my plans and problems as I grow and work out my place and purpose in the world.

For some of us, such an experience of a father is real and true. For others, it is far removed from our experience, and we have little or no understanding of fatherly love or support in our lives. The good news for all of us is that God offers each of us a father relationship with him—no matter our age or station in life. We are created to be like children throughout our lives, in the sense that we will always benefit from the presence, love, and strength of a father. Willingness to trust like a child can easily be lost on the journey through adult life. The love and presence of a father enables us to be complete, secure, and to live with a sense of confidence and purpose.

Separated from God the Father, we quickly sink into dysfunction. We grab hold of power, position, pleasure, and wealth to prove to others that we have value. We desperately adorn the outside of our lives with these trinkets, while the inside grows increasingly hollow and empty.

If you doubt that truth, just ask your spouse, friends, or children. A hollow man seldom hears the sounds he makes. Jesus said that if we have seen him, we have seen the Father. It is said that the best leaders are those who know how to follow and to serve, and the best fathers (and mothers) are those who allow themselves to be loved and fathered by God.

CONSIDER:

Who is God for you today? Whatever your answer, hear his desire to be a present and loving father for you. All you need to do is invite him.

JOHN 14:23

Jesus replied, "Anyone who loves me will obey my teaching. My Father will love them, and we will come to them and make our home with them."

94 | You Could be the Next Dancing Dog

This is a lighthearted musing that I hope will inspire, particularly if you're feeling life is a bit of a dog today and you're chained in the kennel somewhere...

In case you missed it, a dog named Pudsey won Britain's Got Talent in 2012 together with Ashleigh, his teenage trainer. As they pranced around the stage, the audience watched, mesmerized by the clever, cool little canine dancing around on his hind legs. It certainly was entertaining. Part of the reason was the chemistry between Ashleigh and her pooch, and the fact that she was able to train Pudsey to venture way beyond the comfort zone of most four-legged creatures.

The response people had to the dog and trainer routine was absolute awe and wonder at what Pudsey was capable of—how he "appeared so human and responsive" working in synch with Ashleigh. "I've never seen anything like it," some exclaimed as they applauded with delight. And we thought that dogs could fetch tennis balls and sticks, go for walks, keep us company, bark at strangers, and that was that.

Most of us "dogs" do not get to dance and play, perform, and show off our skills to an adoring crowd like Pudsey did. The vast majority of us subsist far below what is possible because we never encounter someone like Ashleigh who will put in the time to enable us to reach beyond and become... unbelievable. Show me a person living apart from God and I'll show you a gross underachiever. "Rubbish," you retort. "Look at the morning news and what Mark has done with Facebook, or Paul McCartney has achieved in music..." and so on. To which I reply, "You're right, they have been incredibly successful—in a God-less environment where success is measured by the acquisition of dollars. Adoring fans pour out time, money, and passion, desperately desiring someone to be their god or role model." All this begs the question of how do we measure success and whom do we look up to? I'm not saying that everything Mark does is bad or that Facebook is wrong or that Paul writes lousy music.

We are designed and intended for much more than survival, fetching sticks, and "being good" or, by cultural standards, being independently wealthy and successful. "What good is it for someone to gain the whole world, yet forfeit their soul?" (Mark 8:36). The Christian life is meant to be an adventure with Jesus in whose company we discover that we are capable of so much more than we could ever ask or imagine. Pudsey loved doing his routine with Ashleigh. Their mutual success was totally dependent upon their relationship, trust, and fun in one another's company. It was from such a foundation that the performance grew and became a winning combination.

The same is true for us. God doesn't stand over us like a ferocious ringmaster with a whip, screaming instructions. He has no desire to see us "do tricks" either. But he certainly invites us to enter the abundant life he revealed in Jesus and gives promises of hope to anyone who follows him, on earth as in heaven. He wants to encourage us to venture beyond our comfort zones to experience what he/God (our trainer) can release in us and through us with a little practice and training. Except this is not entertainment; it is hearing God speak, healing the sick, encouraging those who are lost, and sharing the love and joy of the Father into a broken world.

CONSIDER:

The miracle of Jesus is that he releases amazing things through any who say, "Here I am, use me." We don't have to be exceptional, just available. If a dancing dog gets our attention, God will even speak through Pudsey. I hope you've been inspired to not settle for less; there's so much more for you too! But it does take time, practice, lots of love, and a willingness to try and to accept your mistakes along the way. Have fun! Don't be shy to find a trainer, or to walk alongside someone who is doing something you would love to do in the future.

LUKE 1:30–38

But the angel said to her, "Do not be afraid, Mary; you have found favor with God. You will conceive and give birth to a son, and you are to call him Jesus. He will be great and will be called the Son of the Most High. The Lord God will give him the throne of his father David, and he will reign over Jacob's descendants forever; his kingdom will never end."

"How will this be," Mary asked the angel, "since I am a virgin?"

The angel answered, "The Holy Spirit will come on you, and the power of the Most High will overshadow you. So the holy one to be born will be called the Son of God. Even Elizabeth your relative is going to have a child in her old age, and she who was said to be unable to conceive is in her sixth month. For no word from God will ever fail."

"I am the Lord's servant," Mary answered. "May your word to me be fulfilled." Then the angel left her.

95 | Spiritual Battle

Jesus and satan work in totally opposite directions.

Light and darkness, life and death, freedom and captivity, affirmation and accusation, unity and division, joy and despair, health and sickness... and on and on. The good (Jesus) and the evil (satan) from within them pours out over those around them, and to whomever they influence. We can discern the company we keep and the voices we listen to by paying attention to what pours out of us. It is never nothing! Words and actions showcase our heart to the world.

Another example of how to tell the difference between the call of Jesus and the call of satan is to pay attention to the call itself. When Jesus called his disciples, he spoke to individuals and invited them one by one into relationship—with him and a bunch of others they may not have known before. He called them to walk together to become his disciples (plural), to travel wherever he went, to do whatever he told them, and to ask any questions. Jesus places himself at the center.

The call of satan draws individuals out of relationship into isolation; it encourages them to mistrust and travel alone. He intimidates and inhibits them from asking "silly" questions in front of others who will think they are stupid. Satan places *us* at the center: let *my* will be done and *my* kingdom come. He tries to convince us that we know best and would be a great god, knowing full well that as we try we will lose our way. And he loves the lost as his captives.

Because we live in a broken world, most of us are conditioned to believe that the ways of the world (deeply influenced by satan's tactics) are normal. Isolation, mistrust, disillusionment, personal preference, political correctness, and a host of other rotten fruit warp and disfigure our view of community. It is the opposite of what Jesus calls us into—but his way feels so counterintuitive somehow. This is why Paul (who for years was deceived) wrote that we would not be outwitted by satan, for we are not ignorant of his designs (2 Corinthians 2:11).

One of the fundamental keys to Christian growth is to learn how to discern the source of the voices we listen to. A significant component in that discernment is walking with other disciples whom Jesus has called and who travel with us. We do not always get to self-select—and often therein lies the treasure, the mystery, and the breakthrough.

In his book *The Four Loves*, C.S. Lewis wrote:

> *To love at all is to be vulnerable. Love anything and your heart will be wrung and possibly broken. If you want to make sure of keeping it intact you must give it to no one, not even an animal. Wrap it carefully round with hobbies and little luxuries; avoid all entanglements. Lock it up safe in the casket or coffin of your selfishness. But in that casket, safe, dark, motionless, airless, it will change. It will not be broken; it will become unbreakable, impenetrable, irredeemable. To love is to be vulnerable.*

CONSIDER:

Here are some common lies rampant in our culture juxtaposed with Jesus' teaching:

God is many things; if you're sincere and a good person, that's what matters.

"I am the way and the truth and the life. No one comes to the Father except through me." (John 14:6)

I would say I'm a Christian and I believe in Jesus . . . but it's private.

In the same way, let your light shine before others, that they may see your good deeds and glorify your Father in heaven. (Matthew 5:16)

I believe in Jesus, but I do not believe in the church.

"And I tell you that you are Peter, and on this rock [Peter's declaration that Jesus is Messiah] I will build my church, and the gates of Hades will not overcome it." (Matthew 16:18)

God helps those who help themselves.

"I am the vine; you are the branches. If you remain in me and I in you, you will bear much fruit; apart from me you can do nothing." (John 15:5)

I would go to church but haven't found the right one for me.

"Jerusalem, Jerusalem, you who kill the prophets and stone those sent to you, how often I have longed to gather your children together, as a hen gathers her chicks under her wings, and you were not willing." (Matthew 23:37)

I would attend church but the people irritate me.

"A new command I give you: Love one another. As I have loved you, so you must love one another. By this everyone will know that you are my disciples if you love one another." (John 13:34-35)

Only a fool tests the water's depth with both feet.

GHANAIAN PROVERB

96 | Underestimating Small

THE ROMAN EMPIRE WAS among the most powerful economic, cultural, political, and military forces in the world of its time. It was one of the largest empires in world history. At its height under Trajan (AD 98–117; it expanded after the life, death, and resurrection of Jesus), it covered 5 million square kilometres. It held sway over an estimated 70 million people, at that time 21 percent of the world's population. The longevity and vast extent of the empire ensured the lasting influence of the Latin and Greek languages, cultures, religions, inventions, architecture, philosophy, law, and forms of government.

"In those days Caesar Augustus issued a decree that a census should be taken of the entire Roman world. (This was the first census that took place while Quirinius was governor of Syria.) And everyone went to his own town to register" (Luke 2:1–3). That is why Mary and Joseph began their journey to Bethlehem, where Jesus would be born in fulfilment of the prophecy uttered by Micah (see below) seven hundred years earlier.

The Roman world was overwhelming in presence and power, ruling with absolute control and military might. In this context, the idea of God being "greater and more powerful" would have seemed impossible, even a joke. Yet in the two verses quoted above and below, his lordship over all is demonstrated by earmarking a tiny town for the birth of his son and utilizing the politics of Rome to accomplish his purposes (unbeknown to them, of course).

The life of Jesus marks an astounding moment in history that changed everything about humanity and yet was, initially, so infinitesimally small and hidden that few thought anything of it. Much more than the first flicker of a commercial lightbulb under the gaze of Thomas Edison, or the mold containing penicillin that turned the tide of infection first noted by

Alexander Fleming, Jesus' life, death, and resurrection sent shockwaves that have been reverberating for over two thousand years.

But it did not happen overnight. The influence of Christianity gradually undermined and overcame the power of Rome, but it took hundreds of years. It helps to remember that.

We are used to quick fixes to our problems. When things don't work out as we want them to, *when* we want them to, we become frustrated, spending yet more time, and money, seeking out even quicker solutions. But the transformation of the human heart, as we all can attest to personally, is seldom an overnight "miracle"; it is a gradual softening, like light filtering through a chink that brightens as the blinds are pulled.

We have been playing with our solutions and changes for as long as we've lived in communities. Our solutions are called political change, our wisdom is from the popular vote, and our gods are politicians offering radical change. Democracy is our best model, yet we struggle to make it work. Leadership is fickle, and the promises of yesterday become the disappointments of today as the next ruling party crumbles beneath the burden of governance.

"Pedestals are for statues not for people," I read recently, which leads me to conclude that when Jesus was talking about a rock and foundation upon which to build and live a life, it was more than a quaint idea. Recognizing the frailty and fickleness around us, he was inviting us to trust God and stand on his promises and revelation as the basis for our values and truth. And that usually begins as a seed and takes time to grow strong and tall.

CONSIDER:

Is what you spend your time, money, and passion on every day important and significant? How do you know? It is easy to imagine greatness in terms of wealth and fame when lasting value may be hidden in the everyday. Maybe it is time to change our lenses. Be careful not to dismiss the small things that you may be involved with; they are not insignificant. Who knows where they may lead?

MICAH 5:2

"But you, Bethlehem Ephrathah, though you are small among the clans of Judah, out of you will come for me one who is ruler over Israel, whose origins are from of old, from ancient times."

A sense of humor is the pole that adds balance to our steps as we walk the tightrope of life.

ARABIC PROVERB

---

97 | The Professor and the Sandbox

Once upon a time a baby was born, the same as millions and millions of others around the world. He was nurtured and raised in a good home (unlike millions and millions around the world) and received the benefits of a loving family, lots of friends, and the best education money could buy. His parents were immensely proud of their only son. "We love you, support you, and are right behind you. Explore the world and make the most of your life, privilege, and opportunities," they told him.

The boy grew into manhood and attended an elite university, applied himself well, worked hard, and eventually chose a path of academic study and research as a professor. He studied stars and galaxies, planets and moons, black holes, how asteroids are born, and how one could explore deeper into the vastness of the "world up there and far away." He became extremely knowledgeable and famous. The proudest moment of his life was having a star named after him. He received a prestigious award for his contributions to research and the development of human understanding of the universe. He beamed on the podium, overflowing with gratitude for his parents and fellow researchers and their love and support through all the years.

Eventually, as is the path of all humanity, the final whistle was blown, the curtain dropped, his last breath fell from his lips like crumpled silk—and he died.

It was only then that he looked down on his life and saw his whole world confined to a paradigm, no bigger than a sandbox floating in the infinity of space. There was so much more beyond—he had no idea! He began to feel ridiculously small and rather stupid. He was like a kid who had spent his entire life trying to construct the perfect sandcastle. Finally, he did. "I cracked it!" he shouted with pride, awaiting the applause. Silence followed; no one was looking and very few cared.

Then a figure appeared before him whom he had vague recollections of meeting as a child. But this person was unlike anyone he'd ever encountered before. All the knowledge and wisdom he'd built his life and identity upon—his sense of purpose and meaning—evaporated. Though he'd set and marked thousands of final examination papers, he was ill prepared. *I didn't anticipate this*, he thought, his heart pounding.

"Do you love me?"

The question hung in the air.

CONSIDER:

This is not intended as a threatening musing but merely an anecdote to place life in perspective. What do you see as you look back on your life so far? There's always good, bad, and perhaps ugly. God has grace for all of it. How do you answer the final question (remember, it's not about being perfect, or the size of your intellect)?

MATTHEW 16:26–27

"For whoever wants to save their life will lose it, but whoever loses their life for me will find it. What good will it be for someone to gain the whole world, yet forfeit their soul? Or what can anyone give in exchange for their soul?"

98 | I Now Realize

CORNELIUS WAS A ROMAN Centurion—a Gentile, not a Jew. He ate pork and never entered a synagogue. He was not one of "God's chosen people."

Despite that fact, there came a day when Cornelius received a word from God (who the Jews thought was "theirs") instructing him to invite Simon Peter to his home. The next day shortly before men arrived at Peter's door, Peter had a vision in broad daylight. It was a large sheet full of animals that he was commanded to kill for food. Peter protested and identified the animals as unclean according to Jewish law and tradition. "Do not call anything impure that God has made clean," came the retort (Acts 10:15).

Then Peter, like Cornelius, received a word from God about an impending request from a Gentile for a visit, and he was instructed to accompany them. A day later, after a long journey by foot, Peter stood among Gentiles in the Centurion's home—a radical action casting all tradition and prejudice aside in obedience to God. They proceeded to share their experiences of the same God. It was a revelation to Peter that cut through tradition, culture, mindsets, and deep prejudice.

In great humility, Peter's opening sentence was, "I now realize how true it is that God does not show favoritism . . . " (Acts 10:34).

One of the most encouraging and attractive things about Peter is that we can relate so easily to him, precisely because his struggles are ours. Despite his many misunderstandings, Jesus never abandoned him or humiliated him in his struggle to make sense of the impossible. There were quite a few moments when Simon Peter muttered, "I now realize . . . " Perhaps it was these eureka moments that formed Peter's deep understanding of God's nature and love. It eventually led to him being able to hear and obey God's heart for the Gentiles. He could not have been used there if he had not worked through all the other "moments," such as:

- I now realize . . . this man called Jesus is not ordinary (after the miraculous catch of fish when they first met and Jesus called Simon to follow him).
- I now realize . . . that Jesus does miraculous healing (after witnessing Jesus heal his sick mother-in-law).
- I now realize . . . that Jesus is unpredictable, compassionate, and practical (after witnessing the feeding of the five thousand).
- I now realize . . . that Jesus honors me when I take risks and will be there when I sink (after stepping out of the boat and walking on water with him).
- I now realize . . . that Jesus lives in absolute peace and trust in his Father's faithfulness (when the disciples were terrified of a storm and Jesus slept in the boat before calming the wild sea).
- I now realize . . . that Jesus' prophetic words that I will be a "rock" are beyond what I believe about myself (after Jesus declared that Simon's name would be Peter).
- I now realize . . . that I haven't seen or understood anything yet (after standing on the Mount of Transfiguration with James, John, Moses, and Elijah and Jesus in all his glory).
- I now realize . . . that my solutions, despite my passion, are not always how Jesus acts (after cutting off a Roman soldier's ear with a sword in Gethsemane).
- I now realize . . . that I'm not as spiritual as I imagined (after falling asleep when Jesus asked for prayer in Gethsemane).
- I now realize . . . that I totally overestimate my strength and ability to follow Jesus (after Peter denied Jesus three times as he approached crucifixion).
- I now realize . . . that no matter how I fail, Jesus will forgive and never abandon me (after Jesus met him on the shores of Galilee and said, "Do you love me?")
- I now realize . . . that I am totally dependent upon Jesus and his Spirit alive in me (after waiting in Jerusalem and being filled with the Holy Spirit at Pentecost).

- I now realize ... that God can use me just like I witnessed him using Jesus (after he and John healed the crippled man at the temple gate).
- I now realize ... that God's Spirit can flow through me with power, give me courage, and set me free to be the rock I never imagined three years ago (after Peter spoke and three thousand were baptized).

There were probably many times Peter was tempted to "unfollow Jesus," and no doubt every one of the disciples shared this sentiment. Ironically, those were the very moments when God wanted to break through and enable Peter to realize something about Jesus, or himself, that would help him grow into a better version of himself.

Conflict is not when we have differing points of view; it is when we allow the expression of differences to sabotage relationships and to release judgment, blame, and name calling.

CONSIDER:

Let us embrace the moments of confusion, misunderstanding, even frustration and be open to what God has for us just beyond. Most often real transformation and growth takes place during life, not merely in our heads or by clicking "like" on Facebook. "I now realize ... " must be on the lips of every disciple of Jesus. Following Jesus includes many moments of not understanding. Be encouraged; your next "I now realize" moment may be just around the corner.

LUKE 18:34

The disciples did not understand any of this. Its meaning was hidden from them, and they did not know what he was talking about.

99 | After the Silence

IMAGINE A CONVERSATION BETWEEN two people and God around the time of the first Christmas.

Four hundred years of silence. Nothing.

From the final words in the last book of the Old Testament until the first words of the New Testament—four hundred years and counting. Malachi ended with a promised declaration about turning the hearts of parents to their children and the hearts of children to their parents. What a great promise . . . must be for next week, or next year. Four hundred years!?

"Why did it take you so long, God?"

"Maybe it took that long before I could get your attention? Perhaps it's more to do with you than it is with me." There's a thought.

Four hundred years of silence, waiting, listening, resignation, anger, despair, giving up, presuming that God's dead.

Four hundred years . . . no sound.

"Did you hear that?"
"What?"
"Listen."
"God's speaking."
"How do you know?"
"Angels appeared announcing his coming to earth, just when we thought . . . "
"Sounds scary. I'm nervous—no, terrified."
"So were the shepherds. Who'd of thought they'd be told?"
"Listen."
"What's he saying?"

"Don't know; the voice is very faint, can't make out the words."
"It's getting louder . . . "
"What's he saying, for God's sake!"
"Nothing much."
"What do you mean? Four hundred years of silence and then nothing?"
"No, it's not nothing. It's just that the sound is not words; it's a baby crying."
"You must be kidding! The first sound of God after four hundred years is a crying baby?"
"Why? Surely he has something to say that we can understand?"
"Or perhaps we don't need to understand. What if the crying baby is more about his presence with us, rather than more information? We'll just argue anyway."
"After four hundred years God speaks by being born as a baby among us?"
"Who'd have thought? People are afraid of God, but not of babies. Do you think he's trying to say something?"
"Maybe . . . 'Do not be afraid. I am here for you. Not against you.' I don't know, it's weird."
"Hope we don't have to wait another four hundred years to hear what he has to say."
"No, I don't think so. Let's watch and see—and listen."

That first Christmas was so unexpected, vastly different, hard to comprehend, but it unlocked the door. God has never been the same since, and neither need we.

CONSIDER:

Sometimes our expectations about what God needs to do, and when, get in the way of hearing and seeing him today. His ways are different. Perhaps this is an opportunity to invite him to speak in an unexpected way, and to help you hear with new ears and see with new eyes.

COLOSSIANS 1:27

To them God has chosen to make known among the Gentiles the glorious riches of this mystery, which is Christ in you, the hope of glory.